THE
ULTIMATE
CANADIAN
SPORTS
TRIVIA BOOK
VOLUME II

The Ultimate Canadian Sports Trivia Book
Volume II

Edward Zawadzki

THE DUNDURN GROUP
TORONTO

Copy-Editor: Lloyd Davis
Design: Andrew Roberts
Printer: Transcontinental

Library and Archives Canada Cataloguing in Publication

Zawadzki, Edward
The ultimate Canadian sports trivia book : volume II / Edward Zawadzki.

ISBN 1-55002-529-5

1. Sports—Canada—History—Miscellanea. I. Title.

GV585.Z393 2004   796'.0971   C2004-904893-7

1   2   3   4   5   08   07   06   05   04

  Canada

ONTARIO ARTS COUNCIL
CONSEIL DES ARTS DE L'ONTARIO

We acknowledge the support of the **Canada Council for the Arts** and the **Ontario Arts Council** for our publishing program. We also acknowledge the financial support of the **Government of Canada** through the **Book Publishing Industry Development Program** and **The Association for the Export of Canadian Books**, and the **Government of Ontario** through the **Ontario Book Publishers Tax Credit** program, and the **Ontario Media Development Corporation's Ontario Book Initiative**.

Care has been taken to trace the ownership of copyright material used in this book. The author and the publisher welcome any information enabling them to rectify any references or credit in subsequent editions.

J. Kirk Howard, President

Photographs used in this book courtesy of The Canadian Baseball Hall of Fame, The Canadian Boxing Hall of Fame, The Canadian Sports Hall of Fame, and The Naismith Museum and Hall of Fame.
Front cover (left to right): Karen Magnussen, Sandy Hawley, Sandy Langford, Bernie "Boom Boom" Geoffrion (centre)
Back cover: (left to right): Jake Gaudaur and Tony Gabriel, Cindy Nicholas, Russ Jackson

Printed and bound in Canada
Printed on recycled paper

www.dundurn.com

Dundurn Press
8 Market Street
Suite 200
Toronto, Ontario, Canada
M5E 1M6

Gazelle Book Services Limited
White Cross Mills
Hightown, Lancaster,
England LA1 4X5

Dundurn Press
2250 Military Road
Tonawanda NY
U.S.A. 14150

This book is dedicated to the memory of my big brother Richard Zawadzki, 1954–2003 — my first hero in life. I know that you didn't really share my love of sports but you certainly believed in the history and traditions that go with it. I miss the chuckles from the private jokes that only brothers can share. We miss you every day. You're always in our hearts.

To my mom Wanda who is a true inspiration to us all. She has taught us more about love and courage than we ever thought possible. Our family's greatest treasure.

To my oldest brother George, words can't tell you how much I love you. You truly are a gift from God.

TABLE OF CONTENTS

ACKNOWLEDGEMENTS

I really am so lucky to have such great friends who stick with me, even during the times when I really don't deserve it. Much thanks and love to George Chuvalo and his lovely Joanne, Dave Bailey, Anthony and Dianne DiFlorio, Victor Mitic, John Grieveson, Bruce Macarthur, Dr. Vincent, Janet and Mike O'Hara, Joelle, Doctors Marvin Sazant and Mory Gutman, Tim Cook (wherever the hell you are), Steve Buffery, Patricia Duffy, Mick and Martin McNamara, Tom and Jill Peckham, Ross Sinclair and Stash. I know there's more of you but I only have so much space.

Yes, Rebecca, you do deserve a raise.

To my lovely and talented niece Jessica Ross.

To all my friends at Dundurn, especially my editor, Barry Jowett, to whom I owe so much.

As always, to my late uncle, Ernie Fedoryn, who always had faith in me.

To Allen Stewart, Jackson, and all the great people at the Canadian Sports Hall of Fame. It truly is one of Canada's greatest treasures. Please admire and support it.

To the *Toronto Sun* and Julie Kirsh — thank you for all your help and support.

To the Canadian Baseball Hall of Fame, the Canadian Football League, the Canadian Boxing Hall of Fame and the James Naismith Museum.

And to Terry Fox

BASEBALL

1. Who was the first Canadian to pitch a major-league no-hitter?

A. Toronto-born Dick Fowler achieved this Canadian first when, as a member of the Philadelphia Athletics, he shut down the St. Louis Browns 1–0. Ironically this game was Fowler's first after an absence of more than two years, during which he served in the Canadian army during World War II. A solid performer during his 10-year career, this athlete had a very respectable win-loss record of 66–79 with an ERA of 4.11. He passed away in 1972 at the young age of 51 and was inducted posthumously into the Canadian Baseball Hall of Fame.

Dick Fowler

2. Who was the first Canadian ever to play major-league baseball?

A. That honour rests with Bill Phillips, a native of Saint John, New Brunswick, who on May 1, 1879, took the field as a member of the Cleveland Blues. Phillips played for Cleveland, Brooklyn and Kansas City during his solid 10-year major-league career. Playing in a total of 1,038 career games, he had a terrific total of 1,130 hits and a career batting average of .266. Phillips passed away in 1900 at the very young age of 43.

3. Who was the first Canadian to win 20 games in one season in the major leagues?

Russell Ford

A. It was Brandon, Manitoba's favourite son, Russell Ford, who did the deed in 1910 when, as a member of the New York Highlanders (who in a couple of years would become known by their current nickname, the Yankees), he racked up an incredible 26–6 record. Playing in an era when the spitball and other pitching trickery were still legal, Ford admitted years after he retired that he had used an emery board from time to time to scuff the ball, making it that much harder to hit. Over a total of only seven major-league seasons, Ford retired with a fantastic won-lost record of 99–71, along with an equally respectable 2.59 ERA. Ford was inducted into the Canadian Baseball Hall of Fame in 1989.

4. Who was the first Canadian to win the coveted Cy Young Award?

A. One of the most dominant pitchers of his generation, Ferguson Jenkins won the 1971 award for the National League with a stellar 24–13 record as a member of the Chicago Cubs. Besides winning the Cy Young, this Chatham, Ontario, native put together seven 20-win seasons, played in three All-Star Games and recorded more than 3,000 strikeouts. He had over 100 wins in both the National and American League and pitched 49 shutouts. He finished his career with a total of 284 wins and a 3.34 ERA. Our great Fergie was inducted into the Canadian Baseball Hall of Fame in 1987, and the Baseball Hall of Fame in Cooperstown in 1991.

5. Who was the second Canadian ever to win the Cy Young Award?

A. It only took thirty-two years before a second Canadian won the Cy Young Award. Montreal-born Eric Gagne, who broke in with the National League's Los Angeles Dodgers in 1999, won the award in 2003 when, as a reliever, he recorded an impressive 55 saves (in 55 chances) while sporting a minuscule 1.20 ERA. This young righthander is still in the early stages of his career, so many more honours should await him.

6. How many Cy Young Awards have been won by Toronto Blue Jays pitchers?

A. In the eight seasons from 1996 until 2003, Blue Jays pitchers were first and foremost, winning four Cy Youngs. Pat Hentgen kicked off the trend in 1996 with a 20–10 record and a 3.22 ERA. Then, in 1997 and '98, the legendary Rocket, Roger Clemens, won back-to-back trophies — he went 21–7, 2.05 in '97 and 20–6, 2.65 in '98. Last, but definitely not least, young Roy Halladay has emerged as one of the finest pitchers in the game, and he won the Cy Young in 2003 with a 22–7 record and a 3.25 ERA.

7. Who were the only two Canadian brothers to play for the Toronto Blue Jays?

A. Toronto-born-and-bred Rob and Rich Butler have been mainstays of Canadian baseball for the better part of a decade. Older brother Rob first took the field as a Blue Jay on June 12, 1993. In 1993, '94 and '99 he logged a total of 109 games. Rich appeared in a grand total of seven games with the Jays before putting in parts of two more seasons in Tampa Bay. Both Butlers have played for the Canadian national team and for the Toronto Maple Leafs of southern Ontario's Intercounty League.

8. Who was the first Canadian player to play for a Canadian major-league team?

A. In the Montreal Expos' inaugural season of 1969 they acquired right-handed relief pitcher Claude Raymond from the Atlanta Braves. Raymond, who hails from St-Jean, Quebec, debuted in the major leagues in 1959 with the Chicago White Sox. En route to Montreal, he also played for the Braves during their days in Milwaukee and represented the Houston Astros at the 1966 All-Star Game. He put in three seasons with the Expos before retiring after the 1971 season. He had a career record of 46 wins and 53 losses with 83 career saves.

9. Who was the only Montreal Expo to win a Cy Young Award?

A. Pedro Martinez has become a dominant force in baseball, winning a total of three Cy Youngs so far in a career that started with the L.A. Dodgers in 1992. After signing with the Expos in 1994, where he spent the next four seasons, he really blossomed. It was in 1997 that Pedro won his first Cy Young, when he put together an impressive 17–8 record with a 1.90 ERA and 305 strikeouts in an Expos uniform. Unfortunately, after that season Martinez went to the Boston Red Sox in search of greener pastures and further greatness. In his four Montreal seasons, Pedro won a total of 55 games against only 33 losses.

10. Who hit the very first home run in Toronto Blue Jays history?

A. It happened in the expansion Blue Jays' very first game, at Toronto's old Exhibition Stadium, on the afternoon of April 7, 1977. The snow was falling as Anne Murray sang the national anthem, and it kept falling, and blowing around, for the first three innings. In the bottom of the first, Chicago starter Ken Brett struck out John Scott and Hector Torres. Then, Doug Ault, a six-foot three-inch first baseman from Beaumont, Texas, slugged the ball over the fence. Not only that, but two innings later, in his very next time at bat, he repeated the feat. The Jays went on to beat the White Sox, 9–5. The 27-year-old Ault, who had played his rookie season just the year before with the Texas Rangers, appeared in only 256 major-league games, all but nine of them with the Blue Jays.

11. Why is the name of Joseph Lannin significant in baseball history?

A. This native of Lac Beauport, Quebec, was born into an impoverished background, but his always-ambitious nature drove him to move to Boston, where, over the years, he became an extremely wealthy man in the real estate and commodity markets. In 1914, he embarked on a new venture when he bought the Boston Red Sox of the American League. One of his first matters of business was to purchase a young pitcher by the name of Babe Ruth from the minor-league Baltimore Orioles. This transaction paid off almost immediately as the Sox won back-to-back World Series in 1915 and '16. Lannin sold the club a few years later and became well known across the country for his philanthropic work. He has been inducted into the Canadian Baseball Hall of Fame.

12. Which player was named the Canadian baseball player of the half-century in 1950?

A. London, Ontario's own George "Moon" Gibson, who accomplished much in his stellar career as a player and manager. He broke into the major leagues in 1905 with the Pittsburgh Pirates, where he stayed for twelve of his fourteen major-league seasons. A big man (nearly six feet and 190 pounds), he was a surprisingly light-hitting catcher who made up for his offensive shortcomings with one of the best fielding averages in the game. After retiring as a player in 1918, he made his managerial debut in 1920 with his old club, guiding the Pirates to a second-place finish a year later. He also spent part of 1925 as the field boss of the Chicago Cubs, and reclaimed the helm in Pittsburgh in 1932. He last managed in 1934. He died in London in 1967, at the age of 86. He is a member of the Canadian Sports Hall of Fame.

13. What native of Hamilton, Ontario, broke into the majors as a 17-year-old shortstop?

A. Frank "Blackie" O'Rourke made his move into the bigs in 1912, when he played 61 games for the Boston Braves. Demoted at the end of the season, he vowed that he would make it back to the major leagues someday. He finally made it back with the Brooklyn Robins (later the Dodgers) in 1917 and stayed in baseball for the next 60 years as a player and scout. He retired as a player in 1931 with a .254 hitting average, having played for Washington, the Boston Red Sox, the Detroit Tigers and the St. Louis Browns. His best year was in Detroit in 1925, when he hit .293 with 40 doubles and 29 steals. After retiring, he became a major-league scout for over 40 years with both the Cincinnati Reds and New York Yankees. Blackie passed away in 1986 at the ripe old age of 91.

14. Which Canadian-born baseball rookie phenom was the son of an NHL All-Star?

A. Born in Montreal in 1939, Pete Ward made quite the impression on the baseball world in 1963. As the rookie third baseman for the Chicago White Sox, he led the team in runs, hits, homers, RBI, doubles, batting average, slugging percentage and even errors. He was so impressive that he was chosen by *The Sporting News* as the American League rookie of the year. Athletic prowess must run in the Ward family; Pete's dad, Jimmy, was a two-time NHL All-Star, in 1934 and '37, with the Montreal Maroons and was part of the Stanley Cup–winning Maroons team in 1935. Unfortunately, Pete's career was hampered by injuries and he retired in 1970. He had a solid .254 career batting average and hit 98 homers in his 973 major-league games.

15. Which Canadian pitcher made his major-league debut in 1941 at the age of 33?

A. Oscar "Lefty" Judd was born in Rebecca, Ontario, a small hamlet just outside London. After bouncing around the minor leagues for several years, Judd finally got his chance with the 1941 Boston Red Sox. His best season was in 1943, when, with a record of 11–6, he was chosen for the American League All-Star team. Always a good-hitting pitcher, he had a career .262 average and was often used as a pinch hitter. In 1949, he went to Toronto to play in the International League, and pitched a no-hitter against Syracuse. He died in 1995, at 87, in Ingersoll, Ontario. Judd is a member of the Canadian Baseball Hall of Fame.

16. Which Toronto Blue Jays manager was fired for lying about his military exploits?

A. Tim Johnson was a relatively unknown commodity when he was hired as skipper of the 1998 Blue Jays. A former utility infielder, he played parts of seven major-league seasons, including Toronto in 1978 and '79. In '98, he led the team to a very respectable 88–74 season, good for third place in the American League's East Division. Shortly thereafter, stories circulated about Johnson trying to fire up the team by recounting his wartime exploits as a U.S. Marine in Vietnam. As it turned out, Johnson was a Marine reservist, and never did a tour of Vietnam. The team seemed to lose confidence in Johnson, and he was replaced by the veteran bench boss Jim Fregosi for the 1999 season.

17. What Canadian replaced Babe Ruth in the New York Yankees lineup?

A. George Selkirk of Huntsville, Ontario, definitely had some huge shoes to fill when he not only took over the Bambino's place in right field but was assigned his number 3 jersey. Even though he never produced at a Ruthian pace, he put together some impressive stats in his own right, batting .290 over an 846-game career, twice driving in 100 runs, and clubbing a total of 108 home runs. He was also part of five World Series champions. In the 1960s, he became the general manager of the Washington Senators, a post he held down for the better part of a decade.

George Selkirk

18. Who is the only Toronto Blue Jay to win the American League MVP award?

A. It was Dominican-born George Bell who won that honour, in 1987, when he led the Jays with 47 home runs, 134 RBI with an outstanding .308 batting average. This talented and sometimes controversial left fielder spent a total of twelve seasons in the major leagues, nine of them as a member of the Blue Jays. Spending his last three seasons in Chicago, with both the Cubs and White Sox, Bell's career totals stood at 265 home runs, 1,002 RBI and a solid .278 batting average. Since his retirement, Bell has worked as a coach and instructor in the Blue Jays organization.

19. Greg Harris, a pitcher for the Montreal Expos, was the first pitcher in the twentieth century to do what?

A. Greg Harris, a journeyman pitcher who played for eight major-league clubs in his 15-year career (including two tours with Montreal), secured his place in baseball lore at the advanced age of 39. On September 28, 1995, Harris took the mound in the top of the ninth inning of a game against the Cincinnati Reds and shut down the side by pitching as both a righty *and* a southpaw! Throwing with his right hand, he retired the first batter, Reggie Sanders, on a ground out. Next up were a couple of lefthanded bats, Hal Morris and Eddie Taubensee, so Harris switched hands. As a southpaw, he walked Morris, but induced Taubensee to ground out. He reverted to pitching righthanded against Bret Boone, who grounded out to end the inning. The ambidextrous Harris, who had waited his whole career to attempt this feat, finally got the chance in the last season (and second-to-last game) of his career. He wore a specially-designed six-finger reversible glove that had a thumb hole on either side. Harris retired after the 1995 season with a career mark of 74 wins, 90 losses and 54 saves with a 3.69 ERA. He now runs a pitching school in California.

20. What former Blue Jay also became the team's television colour commentator *and* its manager?

A. Buck Martinez is one of those people who can definitely say that he's done just about everything when it comes to the sport of baseball. A student of the game, his baseball insight has made him a much-sought-after analyst on television and radio broadcasts. Martinez was a hard worker who earned a reputation as a good defensive catcher. He broke in with Kansas City in 1969 and, after a stop with the Milwaukee Brewers, joined the Blue Jays in 1981, wearing number 13 and becoming part of a very successful platoon with Ernie Whitt. He was a Jay until his retirement in 1986. Always interested in broadcasting, he was the Jays' TV colour man from 1987 until November 2000, when he was offered the Toronto managerial reins. Thus began a rocky relationship that saw Buck fired midway through his second season, after accumulating a record of 100–115. He then returned to broadcasting, and he is currently doing colour for the Baltimore Orioles.

21. What baseball record does Glen Gorbous of Alberta hold?

A. It wasn't his all-around baseball ability that bought fame to Drumheller, Alberta's Glen Gorbous — just one aspect of a baseball player's skills. On August 1, 1957, he threw a regulation baseball a total of 445 feet, 10 inches, breaking the old record, set four years earlier, by two and a half feet. This feat was recognized by the *Guinness Book of World Records*. Gorbous's own major-league career entailed a total of 117 games over three seasons from 1955–57 with the Philadelphia Phillies and Cincinnati Reds.

22. Who is the only Montreal Expo to win 20 games in a season for the club?

A. The only pitcher to win 20 games solely in a Montreal uniform was Ross Grimsley. In 1978, the lefthander from Topeka, Kansas, finished with a 20–11 record, his best in a major-league career that began in Cincinnati in 1971. Grimsley retired in 1982 with a 124–99 career record and an ERA of 3.81.

Many people claim that there has been a second pitcher who achieved the feat, but Bartolo Colon posted 10 of his 20 wins in 2002 with the Cleveland Indians before a midseason trade to the Expos.

23. Which Canadian ballplayer dominated the sport in 1887?

A. To say that Woodstock, Ontario's James "Tip" O'Neill simply dominated the major leagues that season would not do justice to his accomplishments. With the St. Louis Browns of the American Association, he led the league in home runs (14), batting average (.435), slugging percentage (.691), on-base percentage (.490), runs scored (167), hits (225), RBI (123), doubles (52), and triples (19).

In the 10 full seasons he played in the major leagues with St. Louis, Chicago, New York, and Cincinnati he had a lifetime batting average of .326. He passed away in Montreal, Quebec, in 1915.

24. How many times have Toronto Blue Jays players won the American League Rookie-of-the-Year Award?

A. Since their inception in 1977, the Jays have seen two of their most promising young players win rookie-of-the-year honours. In 1979, shortstop Alfredo Griffin shared the award with John Castino of the Minnesota Twins. This future All-Star and Gold Glove winner was one of the top shortstops in the game for many of his 18 seasons in the majors. It was a long time — 13 years — before another Blue Jay, third baseman Eric Hinske, would win the award. In 2002, the Wisconsin native, who was obtained from the Oakland organization, hit an impressive 24 homers, drove in 84 runs and drew 77 walks.

25. Where did the Montreal Expos first play their home games?

A. When the Expos were first granted their major-league franchise it was with the understanding that, within a few years of their debut in 1969, they would have their own domed stadium in which to play. Until that time, they were to make do with Jarry Park, which then seated only 3,000. A rush to build bleachers and portable seating ensued, and by April of 1969 the capacity had been raised to 28,500. It wasn't until 1977 that the Expos were finally able to move into the much larger Olympic Stadium. In 2003 and 2004, the Expos have played a number of "home" games at Hiram Bithorn Stadium in San Juan, Puerto Rico.

26. To date, who has pitched the only no-hitter in Toronto Blue Jays history?

A. Dave Stieb was, without a doubt, one of the best pitchers in the major leagues throughout the 1980s and early '90s. This California native was called up to the Jays in 1979 and played in Toronto for 15 of his 16 big-league seasons. On September 2, 1990, after a couple of close calls, he finally pitched a no-no, beating the Cleveland Indians 3–0. Two years earlier, he pitched back-to-back one-hitters against the Baltimore and Cleveland on September 24 and 30, 1988. In both of those games, his no-hit bids were foiled with two out in the ninth inning. This seven-time All-Star retired in 1993, then made a brief comeback in '98 before quitting for good with a record of 176–137 and a 3.44 ERA.

27. Can you tell which of these players played professional baseball in Canada?

a) Pete Rose
b) Jackie Robinson
c) Phil Niekro
d) Sparky Anderson

A. Trick question: the answer is all of the above. Rose, the holder of major-league records for most games and most base hits in a career, played a total of 95 games for the Montreal Expos in 1984. Before breaking Major League Baseball's colour barrier, the great Jackie Robinson played the 1946 season with the Montreal Royals — the triple-A affiliate of the Brooklyn Dodgers, the team that Robinson would star with. Niekro, one of the masters of the knuckleball, was acquired by the Blue Jays in August of 1987 for their pennant race with the Detroit Tigers. He started three games for Toronto, losing his only two decisions, before he was released. At 48, he was the oldest player ever to wear a Jays uniform. Anderson was a solid infielder in the early 1960s for the triple-A Toronto Maple Leafs. He then went on to became the team's manager before achieving fame — and World Series championships — at the helm of the Cincinnati Reds and Detroit Tigers.

28. Which major-league player was a member of both the Montreal Expos and the Toronto Blue Jays in their inaugural seasons?

A. It was first baseman/outfielder Ron Fairly, and he not only played for both in their debut seasons, but he appeared in the All-Star Game as a member of both. (He represented the Expos in 1973 and the Jays in '77.) Fairly played for a total of six teams in his 21-year career and hit 215 homeruns while batting for a respectable lifetime average of .266.

29. Which Canadian-born long-time major-league umpire also played in the Canadian Football League?

A. It was Montreal-born-and-raised Jim McKean, who grew up to be a fine multisport athlete. After graduating from Concordia University he joined the Saskatchewan Roughriders as a quarterback, and after retiring from football he turned to baseball officiating. Starting in the low minors in 1970, his rise to the major leagues was rapid — he was in the American League by 1973. During his 28 years in the bigs, he worked three World Series, three All-Star Games and many league and divisional championships. In 2002 he became one of the supervisors of umpires for Major League Baseball. In one of the most comical and unusual officiating moves ever, McKean ejected B.J. Birdy, the Toronto Blue Jays' mascot, from a May 1993 game for making what he believed to be offensive gestures.

30. What is London, Ontario–born Ted Giannoulas's contribution to the sport of baseball?

A. For more than 30 years, Giannoulas has entertained baseball fans as the high-profile San Diego Chicken. As a university student at San Diego State University, he accepted a part-time job with radio station KGB that paid him $2 an hour to hand out Easter eggs to kids visiting the zoo. Little did he know that the job would become his career for more than three decades and take him all over North America as baseball's best-known goodwill ambassador. He has also found himself on stage with the likes of Chuck Berry, the Doobie Brothers, the Ramones and many other rock 'n' roll acts. At one concert he even got the attention of the King, Elvis Presley, while doing his act in the crowd. He still performs roughly 200 shows a year and has been nominated for induction into the Canadian Baseball Hall of Fame.

31. Which former Toronto Blue Jay is currently the manager of Canada's national baseball team?

A. That job is held by a man who is, without a doubt, one of the most popular players ever to don a Blue Jays uniform: Ernie Whitt. The Detroit native was drafted by the Boston Red Sox in 1972, was claimed by Toronto in the 1977 expansion draft, and was the Jays' starting catcher from 1980 until '89. A fair-hitting catcher (especially when platooned with Buck Martinez), Whitt batted .253 for his career, clouted 134 home runs and drove in 531 runs. He retired after spending the 1991 season with the Baltimore Orioles, and has since worked as a coach and instructor in the Blue Jays system. He has enjoyed success as skipper of the national team, guiding the squad to a silver medal at the Americas Olympic Qualifier. As a result, Canada became one of two countries from the region, along with Cuba, that competed at the 2004 Olympics in Athens, Greece.

BASKETBALL

1. Who was the first Canadian woman selected to play in the WNBA All-Star Game?

A. It was Markham, Ontario's own Tammy Sutton-Brown, who played for the Eastern Conference squad in 2002. After starring at Rutgers University — in her final college season, she led the Scarlet Knights with an average of 12.0 points per game and was voted the team's most improved player — she was chosen in the second round of the 2001 draft by the Charlotte Sting. She was only the second Canadian ever drafted in the league's four-year history. In her four WNBA seasons she has become quite a star. She has also, as a member of the Canadian national team, represented Canada at the 2000 Olympics in Sydney. When the WNBA season is over, she plays winter ball for a women's pro league in Korea.

2. Which Canadian NBA player is married to movie star, singer and former Miss America, Vanessa Williams?

A. That would be Toronto-born Rick Fox, whose exploits on the court are also worthy of note. Drafted by the Boston Celtics in the first round in 1991, that fall he became the first Boston rookie to start on opening night since Larry Bird in 1979. Signed by the Los Angeles Lakers in 1997 as a free agent, the six-foot, seven-inch forward has become one of the team's most dependable players, averaging more than 25 minutes per game and boasting a field-goal percentage of .450. Since joining the Lakers, he has been part of three NBA championships.

3. Which Canadian-raised member of the Dallas Mavericks has played in two NBA All-Star Games?

A. Victoria, British Columbia's favourite son, Steve Nash, has become one of the top players in basketball today. As his two All-Star appearances, in 2002 and 2003, show, Nash has developed into an excellent playmaker and three-point shooter who averages close to 30 minutes per game. Chosen 15th overall by the Phoenix Suns in the 1996 draft, this Santa Clara grad was traded to Dallas in 1998, after which his career blossomed. Nash has also given back to his home country by being one of the key members of Canada's national team.

4. Which well-known Canadian player was the youngest ever to compete for the national team?

A. It was Toronto-born Leo Rautins, who played for his country at the tender age of 16. Rautins went on to play for the University of Minnesota, where he made the Big Ten's all-rookie team, before transferring to Syracuse, where the six-foot-eight forward earned All-America honours. Drafted 17th overall by the Philadelphia 76ers in 1983, Rautins played only 32 regular-season games (plus three playoff matches) in the NBA before setting out to play the next several years in the European professional leagues. Unfortunately, Leo had chronic knee problems throughout his career, and he retired in 1992 after his 14th knee operation. He then turned his attention to broadcasting, which he has tackled successfully, working as an analyst for ESPN and being a very capable colour man for the Toronto Raptors.

Leo Rautins

5. Who were the first Canadians to play for a Canadian-based NBA team?

Gino Sovran

A. You'll have to go back nearly 50 years, to the inaugural season of the Toronto Huskies. Back in 1946–47, two talented athletes from the University of Windsor, Hank Biasatti and Gino Sovran, both suited up for the Huskies, a charter member of the Basketball Association of American (it became the NBA in 1949) that lasted only one season before folding. Unfortunately, both players' pro basketball careers ended with the demise of the Huskies, but both would go on to find other sports-related work. Biasatti was a fine baseball player who also played first base with the Philadelphia Athletics in 1949.

6. How many players have won the NBA's Rookie-of-the-Year award while playing for the Toronto Raptors?

A. Since the team's inception in 1995, two Raptors were talented enough to win rookie-of-the-year laurels. The first was Damon Stoudamire, who starred in the inaugural 1995–96 season. Stoudamire, a five-foot, ten-inch guard from the University of Arizona, was drafted seventh overall by Toronto. He electrified the Skydome crowds, averaging 19 points and 40.9 minutes per game. Unfortunately, there was talk that Stoudamire was unhappy in Toronto, and midway through the 1997–98 season he was traded to the Portland Trail Blazers. The second was Vince Carter, who had starred with the University of North Carolina. He was drafted fifth overall in 1998 — by the

Golden State Warriors, who immediately traded Carter and some cash to the Raptors for the rights to Antawn Jamison. Carter quickly developed into a cornerstone of the Raptors franchise, and was named rookie of the year in 1998–99 after averaging 18.3 points per game — which, incidentally, made him the only rookie to lead his team in scoring that season.

7. Which women's basketball star was chosen third overall in the WNBA draft — highest ever for a Canadian?

A. It was Brockville, Ontario's own Stacey Dales-Schuman, the six-foot All-America guard from the University of Oklahoma. After a fantastic college career in which Stacey led her Sooners to the NCAA finals for the first time, she was chosen third overall by the Washington Mystics in the 2002 draft. She quickly made her presence known by being the second-highest scorer on the team and being selected to the All-Star team. She has also become a successful broadcaster who works for both TSN (as a courtside reporter on Raptors games) and ESPN (as an analyst on women's college basketball broadcasts).

8. Can you name all the coaches of the Toronto Raptors, up to and including the 2003–04 season?

A. Brendan Malone got the tough job of being the Raptors' first head coach. The former New York Knicks assistant led the team to a 21–61 season and was fired at the end of the year. Darrell Walker took over in 1996–97, and by the time of his departure in February 1998 he had chalked up a record of 41–90. He was replaced by Butch Carter, who, through the end of the 1999–2000 season, managed a more respectable 73–92 mark, including the Raptors' first winning season (45–37 in 1999–2000) and first playoff appearance (they were swept by the Knicks in the first round in 2000). Lenny Wilkens, who has won (and lost) more games than any other coach in NBA history, became the fourth man to take the helm. After seasons of 47 and 42 wins, the 2002–03 campaign was a disaster, with only 24 wins against 58 losses. His place was taken by Kevin O'Neill, who was fired at the end of 2003–04 (33–49), as was long-time general manager Glen Grunwald.

9. Can you name the first Canadian ever to play in the WNBA?

A. Kelly Boucher of Calgary, Alberta, was first when she suited up for the Charlotte Sting in 1998. She also played for several years in Europe and the Middle East. Always a proud Canadian, she was also a long-time member of the national team, playing at the Olympics in Atlanta and Sydney in 1996 and 2000. This former All-Canadian from the University of Victoria can never be mistaken for a dumb jock: she studied sports medicine and speaks six languages. At last look, she was the president of the board of directors of Basketball Alberta.

10. Which Canadian star was drafted in 2000 by the Charlotte (now New Orleans) Hornets?

A. It was Toronto's own Jamaal Magloire, who, after starring at the University of Kentucky, was drafted in the first round (19th overall). As a sophomore in college, the six-foot, eleven-inch centre set a team record in blocked shots. One of the highest points of this young man's career came in 2004, when he played for the Eastern Conference All-Star Team, becoming only the second Canadian chosen to play in the annual classic. Coming off the bench, Magloire scored 19 points and was truly one of the best players in the game, even though his Eastern Conference team lost 136–132. Many experts believe that he deserved to take player-of-the-game honours.

11. Is there a Canadian Basketball Hall of Fame?

A. There sure is, and it's situated in Almonte, Ontario — the birthplace of James Naismith, the Canadian who invented the game of basketball back in 1891. The hall opened in 1989; the former governor general Roland Michener was its official patron, and the late Jack Donohue, the long-time coach of the Canadian national team, served as its honorary president. There is an annual induction gala, and the hall organizes the annual Naismith Summer Sports Camp for children and teenagers.

The Canadian Basketball Hall of Fame

12. What year did the men's wheelchair basketball team win the Paralympic gold medal?

A. In 2000, at Sydney, Australia. The Canadians won all of their matches leading up to the final, in which they defeated the Netherlands, 57–43. Canada dominated the tournament, leading all teams in points scored, fewest points allowed, blocked shots and field-goal percentage. The Canadian team is one of the favourites in the Athens Games in 2004. In 2000, Canada's women's team won its third straight Paralympic gold medal.

13. How many Canadians have actually played in the NBA?

A. Through the 2003–04 season, there have been 17. (This list doesn't include players who were drafted but did not play in an NBA game.)

1. Norm Baker, Chicago Stags, 1946–47
2. Hank Biasatti, Toronto Huskies, 1946–47
3. Gino Sovran, Toronto Huskies, 1946–47
4. Ernie Vandeweghe, New York Knicks, 1949–56
5. Bob Houbregs, Milwaukee Hawks, Baltimore Bullets, Boston Celtics, Fort Wayne/Detroit Pistons, 1953–58
6. Brian Heaney, Baltimore Bullets, 1969–70
7. Lars Hansen, Seattle Super Sonics, 1978–79
8. Jim Zoet, Detroit Pistons, 1982–83
9. Stewart Granger, Cleveland Cavaliers, Atlanta Hawks, New York Knicks, 1983–87
10. Leo Rautins, Philadelphia 76ers, Atlanta Hawks, 1983–85
11. Ron Crevier, Detroit Pistons, Golden State Warriors, 1985–86
12. Mike Smrek, Chicago Bulls, Los Angeles Lakers, San Antonio Spurs, Golden State Warriors, Los Angeles Clippers, 1985–92

13. Bill Wennington, Dallas Mavericks, Sacramento Kings, Chicago Bulls, 1985–99
14. Rick Fox, Boston Celtics, Los Angeles Lakers 1991–present
15. Steve Nash, Phoenix Suns, Dallas Mavericks, 1996–present
16. Todd MacCulloch, Charlotte/New Orleans Hornets, 2000–present
17. Jamaal Magloire, Charlotte/New Orleans Hornets 2000–present

14. Who coached Canada's men's national team for 17 years ending in 1988?

A. To say that Jack Donohue was just a coach would do a great injustice to the man, his players and the system he played such a large role in developing. For more than a decade he coached high school hoops in New York City, including a dominant squad at Power Memorial that won 71 games in a row. At Power, he tutored the young Lew Alcindor, who as Kareem Abdul-Jabbar became an NBA legend. After Donohue took over the reins of Canada's national team in 1972, the

Jack Donohue

country's stock in the international basketball community began to rise slowly. In 1983, he guided Canada to a gold medal in the World University Games, defeating such powerhouses as the United States and Yugoslavia. A year later, he coached the national team to a fourth-place finish at Olympics in Los Angeles. He retired after the Seoul Olympics in 1998, but still kept a hand in the sport, serving on several advisory boards. He passed away in Ottawa in April 2003.

15. Whatever happened to the Vancouver Grizzlies?

A. After joining the NBA alongside the Toronto Raptors in 1995, the Grizzlies struggled to assemble a team that could win consistently, reaching a low point in the lockout-shortened 1998–99 season, when their 8–42 record was the worst in the league. Fans began to lose patience and corporate support dwindled. A new owner, Michael Heisley, approached the NBA about moving his team, and after an extensive search he decided upon Memphis, Tennessee. The Memphis Grizzlies made their debut on November 1, 2001, losing 90–80 to the Detroit Pistons. Their fortunes finally took a turn for the better in 2003–04, when they won 50 games and made the playoffs.

BOXING

1. How many times has Montreal-born-and-raised Arturo Gatti held a major world title?

A. Without a doubt one of the most exciting boxers ever to climb into the squared circle, Arturo "Thunder" Gatti has held two major world championships. The first was won on December 15, 1995, when he defeated American Tracy Harris Patterson in 12 rounds for the IBF junior lightweight championship, and on January 24, 2004, he defeated Italy's Gianluca Branco for the WBC super lightweight crown. His three gruelling matches with the American "Irish" Micky Ward are among the greatest fights in the annals of the sport, and his "no survivors" style of boxing has rightfully gained him a reputation as boxing's "greatest human highlight film."

2. What Montreal-based boxer won the WBC super middleweight title in 2001?

A. That was Eric Lucas, who claimed the championship on July 10, 2001, when he defeated Glenn Catley. The six-foot, four-inch Quebecer had been unsuccessful in two previous world title shots against American Roy Jones and Fabrice Tiozzo of France. After winning, he made three successful defences of his title before losing a very controversial decision to the German fighter Markus Beyer in the challenger's hometown of Berlin in April 2003. A very methodical fighter who wears his opponents down over time, Lucas says he will work hard to regain the world title that most believe was unfairly taken from him.

3. A Canadian boxer by the name of Lisa Brown achieved something important twice in one year. What was it?

A. "Downtown" Lisa Brown, a former provincial and national champion in 1998 and '99, was born in Trinidad and now calls Toronto her home. Encouraged by her husband Errol, himself a ranked Canadian welterweight, Lisa turned pro in May 2000 and KO'd American Leilani Salazar. Remaining undefeated, on April 27, 2001, she defeated Leona Brown for the IFBA junior featherweight title, and on August 31, just four months later, she defeated the same Leona Brown to win the vacant IWBF bantamweight title.

4. Which Canadian boxing silver medallist came out of the closet after the Olympics?

A. A true fighter both outside and inside the squared circle, Toronto's own Mark Leduc has shown great courage and character in overcoming adversity all his life. The winner of the silver medal in the light welterweight class at the 1992 Barcelona Olympics, Leduc came home and put together a brief but successful career in the professional ranks, winning the Canadian title. It was at that point that Leduc made it public that he was a homosexual. Since his retirement from boxing, he has been active as a social advocate and currently works in the film industry.

5. Which Canadian-based boxer won the WBA lightweight crown in 2002?

A. It was Romanian-born — but Montreal-based — Leonard Dorin who, on January 5, 2002, defeated Raul Horacio Balbi in San Antonio, Texas, to win the world title. Since turning pro in 1998, after he came to Montreal to compete under the watchful eye of Yvon Michel and the Interbox promotional group, Dorin has put together an amazing 22–0–1 record. His one draw was against IBF title holder Paul Spadafora in a title-unification match. On October 24, 2003, when he wasn't able to make weight for a title defence, he relinquished his title to Miguel Callist, saying it would be too difficult to make weight.

6. Who won a world title in Toronto on April 6, 2000, at the Air Canada Centre?

A. In the first pro boxing card ever held at the current home of the Toronto Maple Leafs, Margaret Sidoroff of London, Ontario, beat Para Draine of Washington state in a unanimous decision to win the IWBF world flyweight championship. Margaret, who was also an undefeated national amateur champion with a record of 13–0, now lives in Windsor and trains with the Border City Boxing Club.

7. Has Canadian heavyweight Kirk Johnson ever fought for the heavyweight title?

A. The native of North Preston, Nova Scotia, has had several chances to achieve greatness in the world of pro boxing, but for different reasons he seems to have fallen short of his goals. On July 27, 2002, he met WBA heavyweight champ John Ruiz in a fight that many experts felt should have been a cake-walk for the talented Johnson. The bout was very close, and

Johnson got frustrated with the pace and in-close style and started throwing punches below the belt. Despite warnings from the referee, Johnson kept up the low blows and was disqualified in the 10th round. In December of 2003, Johnson was destroyed by Ukrainian heavyweight Vitali Klitscko in a heavyweight eliminator bout.

8. Which Canadian-based heavyweight champion was knocked out by Mike Tyson?

A. That was Jamaican-born, Halifax-based Trevor Berbick. Berbick had won the WBC championship by defeating American Pinklon Thomas in Las Vegas on March 22, 1986. It was exactly eight months later that Berbick faced the hungry new lion of the sport, 20-year-old Mike Tyson, who aimed to become the youngest man ever to ever win the world heavyweight championship. Once the bell rang it was a one-sided affair with Tyson knocking out Berbick in spectacular fashion in two rounds. Berbick continued to fight for many years, winning some very minor titles, but would never again reach the top.

9. Was Lennox Lewis ever the undisputed heavyweight champion of the world?

A. British-born but raised in Kitchener, Ontario, Lennox won a gold medal for Canada at the 1988 Seoul Olympics by knocking out Riddick Bowe of the United States in the heavyweight final. Their paths would cross again a few years later when Bowe, now the world champion, refused to fight Lewis and was stripped of his title. Lewis then became the dominant heavyweight on the planet. On November 13, 1999, Lewis became the undisputed world champion when he defeated Evander Holyfield in a title unification match that saw Lewis put up his WBC title against Holyfield's IBF and WBA belts.

Lennox Claudius Lewis retired from boxing on February 6, 2004, with an impressive record of 41–2–1.

10. What ex–world champion boxer is the pride of Pugwash, Nova Scotia?

A. Doris Hackl, a two-time national amateur champion, was born in Austria but has called the Maritimes her home for the better part of a decade. After her amateur boxing successes as Canadian champ, she went pro in May 1999 on a boxing card in Halifax. It was less than a year later that the undefeated Canadian decisioned American Chevelle Hallback for the IFBO junior lightweight title. Hackl retired from the ring in 2002 after losing her title to American Brenda Vickers.

11. Which Canadian boxer was known as the Bulldog?

A. Edmonton's own Scotty Olson answered to that very fitting nickname. Standing just five feet tall and weighing 112 pounds, Olson's diminutive frame contained the heart of a giant. Scotty captured the nation's respect and admiration with his exciting standup, take-no-prisoners style of boxing. He proudly represented Canada, winning a gold medal, at the 1986 Commonwealth Games and made it to the quarterfinals at the 1988 Seoul Olympics. Turning pro in 1990, he quickly won the Canadian title and in 1994 captured the IBA flyweight championship, which he held for four years. After fighting injuries for many years, Scotty announced his retirement in 2003. He has stayed busy with the promotional and business side of the sport, and much of his time is taken up by his tireless devotion to charity work.

12. Which Canadian won a silver medal at the 1988 Seoul Olympics?

A. Born in Guyana and raised in Toronto, Egerton Marcus is not only one of the most talented boxers ever developed in Canada, he's also one of the best liked. Competing for Canada at the Seoul Olympics, Marcus lost the middleweight gold medal match to Germany's Henry Maske. After returning home, he signed a promotional deal with Main Events Boxing, a well-known U.S. promotional outfit, and he turned pro in 1989. In 1992, he won the NABF (North American) light heavyweight title with an 11th-round TKO of Art Bayliss. On February 11, 1995, he met with his old adversary, Maske, for the IBF light heavyweight title, but again Maske outpointed the game. Marcus is now retired and is a trainer and gym owner in Toronto. For many years he was also the chief sparring partner for his good friend Lennox Lewis.

13. What did Canadian heavyweight boxer "Wild Bert" Kenney do on July 8, 1916, in New York City?

A. All this native of Prince Edward Island did was battle the legendary Jack Dempsey to a 10-round draw. The action was back and forth, and each fighter had the other on the canvas a couple of times. Dempsey himself was quoted as saying that it was "one of the most brutal fights of my life. I could have sold the blood for 14 dollars." Dempsey was still almost exactly three years from winning the world title from Jess Willard.

14. When was the very first women's boxing match sanctioned by Boxing Canada held?

A. It was in July 1991, in Sydney, Nova Scotia. The two combatants were Thérèse Robitaille of Fredericton, New Brunswick, and Jenny Reid, a criminal lawyer from Kingston, Ontario. Both ladies gave it their all, and Robitaille won the decision in the historic match.

15. Who is known as the "Golden Boy"?

A. Victoria, B.C., native Donny Lalonde got that nickname because of his good looks and his long golden tresses. A victim of abuse as a child, Lalonde has been both a spokesman and advocate against child abuse. A solid boxer with great punching ability, he turned pro on April 24, 1980, in Winnipeg, with a second-round TKO of Ken Nichols. On the way to greatness, he picked up a number of minor titles, including the Canadian light heavyweight championship in 1983. On November 27, 1987, in Port of Spain, Trinidad and Tobago, he knocked out Eddie Davis in the second round and became the WBC's light heavyweight champion. Just under a year later, he lost the title in a ninth-round TKO at the hands of the legendary Sugar Ray Leonard in Las Vegas. Lalonde retired after that fight, but over the years has launched several comebacks, although he never again tasted victory in a world championship bout.

16. What role did Irv Ungerman play in the world of Canadian boxing?

A. Ungerman is a well-known boxing manager, promoter and sports entrepreneur. The owner of All-Canada Sports, he has been involved in many major events ranging from world championship boxing to international hockey tournaments. A poultry magnate who boxed as an amateur in his childhood, he has helped manage the careers of such luminaries as George Chuvalo, Clyde Gray and Donovan Boucher. Always known for his charitable works, he has been honoured by many organizations, including being named B'nai Brith's man of the year.

17. What legendary Canadian boxer fought in every weight division from lightweight to heavyweight in his career?

Sam Langford

A. That was the legendary Sam Langford of Weymouth, Nova Scotia. Over a career that lasted from 1902 until 1926, he fought successfully in every one of those weight categories, but despite his great skills he was never given a chance to fight for a world title. In later years he went blind and was penniless. Friends arranged for him to live in a retirement home, where he passed away in 1956.

18. Which Canadian boxer was presented the Order of Canada in 1998?

A. George Chuvalo is without a doubt one of the most beloved athletes in Canadian history. His bouts with such legends as Muhammad Ali, Joe Frazier and Jerry Quarry made him a household name, and an important part of his legend is the fact that, in 97 professional fights, he was never knocked down. But it was in his personal life where Chuvalo has had his toughest fight. Since the mid-1980s he has suffered unimaginable pain due to the heroin addiction and deaths of three of his four sons and the suicide of his distraught wife. Since that time, George has travelled the country speaking of the dangers of drug use and the importance of family love and high self-esteem. In October of 1998, the Canadian government recognized the importance of George's work by naming him to the Order of Canada.

George Chuvalo

19. Who represented Canada in the heavyweight class at the 1992 Olympics?

A. It was the power-punching Tom "The Bomb" Glesby of Welland, Ontario. Unfortunately, Glesby, who many

45

THE ULTIMATE CANADIAN SPORTS TRIVIA BOOK VOLUME II

experts claim had a style more suited to the pro ranks, lost in the early stages of the tourney. Glesby, a Canadian champion on multiple occasions, decided after Barcelona to turn pro, and debuted in a spectacular fashion with a two-round KO against K.P. Porter. Tom then went on a tear through the competition, winning the Canadian heavyweight championship in 1994.

20. Did two Canadians ever fight in an elimination match for the heavyweight championship of the world?

A. Yes. In London, England, on October 31, 1992, Lennox Lewis faced off against Donovan "Razor" Ruddock in a WBC elimination to determine who would be the next opponent to take on the champ, Riddick Bowe. The two Canadians knew each other quite well, and had even sparred together a few years back. Once the bell rang to start the fight, it was no contest; Lewis demolished Ruddock and knocked him out in the second round. Bowe, it seems, wanted no part of Lewis and relinquished his claim to the title, which was then awarded to Lewis.

21. Did a Canadian boxer ever defend his world championship twice in one day?

A. As impossible as it would be for that to happen today, it certainly occurred on March 28, 1906, in San Diego, California. The heavyweight champion of the world at the time, Hanover, Ontario's own Tommy Burns, had won the title from Marvin Hart a little more than a month before. On this date, he defended his crown against Jim O'Brien and James J. Walker. Even though some records claim that the bouts were exhibition matches, both were sanctioned by the promoter and the press as being for the world championship. Burns had no trouble with either man that day, as he knocked

Tommy Burns

out each one in the first round. Burns would defend his title a total of 17 times in two and a half years years before losing to Jack Johnson in Australia on December 25, 1908.

22. Has Otis Grant ever held a world title?

A. Otis "Magic" Grant, who spent four years as an amateur, turned pro under the watchful eye of his good friend and long-time trainer Russ Anber. Constantly improving and winning minor titles along the way, on December 13, 1997, he decisioned Ryan Rhodes to capture the WBO's world middleweight championship in a bout in England. Then, on November 14, 1998, he faced the biggest test of his career when he met Roy Jones Jr., who was — and still is considered to be — pound for pound the best fighter in the world. Unfortunately, Otis lost his bid for Jones's WBA light heavyweight title. Then, early in 1999, as Grant was driving along the highway with his daughter and another boxer in the car, a vehicle crossed the median and injured all three — especially Otis, who spent a week in a coma and had to undergo extensive rehabilitation. After recovering, he trained some fighters and even dabbled in promotion, but to everyone's surprise, after four and a half years out of the ring, he returned to defeat former world super middleweight champion Dingaan Thobela of Africa.

23. What did Loi Chow of Vancouver achieve in the sport of boxing?

A. Other than embarrassing himself, his only pugilistic achievement was taking part in the first professional mixed-gender boxing match in North America. An American woman boxer by the name of Margaret McGregor had been scheduled to fight a guy by the name of Hector Morales in Seattle on October 9, 1999. A few days before the bout, Morales backed out, and his place was taken by his trainer, Loi Chow — a professional jockey who claimed to have had a couple of fights. Come fight night, it was McGregor who thoroughly roughed up the smaller Chow. At the end of the four rounds, McGregor had won a unanimous 40–36 decision on all three judges' scorecards.

24. Has there ever been an all-female boxing card in Canada?

A. Yes, on March 24, 1999, in Rayside-Balfour, Ontario, just outside of Sudbury. A team of eight elite Canadian female boxers were assembled there to meet a visiting contingent from Sweden. The fighters had all met two years before in Sweden, in what was the first sanctioned women's tournament ever. In the first meeting, Canadians won five of the eight bouts. Women's boxing had come a long way in Canada — in fact, it had been less than a decade since police had threatened to arrest everyone involved in a proposed women's match in Toronto. But on this Wednesday evening in Rayside-Balfour, the two teams each won four of the eight matches.

25. Is there a Canadian Boxing Hall of Fame?

A. The history of Canadian boxing has been entrusted to the capable hands of boxing entrepreneur and historian Jack Harrell. Articles, photographs and memorabilia from over the past century have been collected to educate fans to the rich, fascinating history of Canadian pugilism. The Hall of Fame is located at 782 Yonge Street in Toronto — at one of the most famous intersections in Canada, Yonge and Bloor. In a related note about the Hall, Muhammad Ali was personally inducted on October 20, 2002, as a tribute to his historic matches with his Canadian challenger and now friend, George Chuvalo.

26. Where in Canada are the Olajide brothers from?

A. Michael "Silk" Olajide was born in Liverpool, England, but moved to Vancouver as a child. He was a tremendous boxer whose misfortune it was to compete during what was known as the golden age of the middleweight, when legends such as Sugar Ray Leonard, Tommy "Hitman" Hearns and "Marvelous" Marvin Hagler dominated the division. Michael, who became the WBC's intercontinental champion in 1987, got a shot at the world title on April 28, 1990, when he lost a 12-round decision to the legendary Hearns. His younger half-brother, Tokunbo Olajide, was born in Vancouver and has been on a tear as of late, positioning himself for a crack at a world title. On February 24, 2004, he KO'd Larry Marks in the second round to win the USBA junior middleweight championship.

27. Which Canadian boxer is known simply as "The Kid"?

A. Billy Irwin's left hook has put many more people to sleep than an Ingmar Bergman movie. This power-punching native of Niagara Falls, Ontario, turned pro after the 1992 Olympics in Barcelona and nearly a decade as an amateur. After his pro debut he tore through his opponents and quickly won the Canadian and Commonwealth lightweight titles. After some managerial setbacks and an ill-advised move to Toronto, Billy moved back to the Falls, got together with his old trainer and mentor, and forged an alliance with Russell Peltz, the famed promoter at Philadelphia's Blue Horizon. With some impressive wins stateside, he put himself in position to fight IBF lightweight Paul Spadafora. They faced off on December 16, 2000, and, unfortunately, Spadafora's style frustrated Billy, who lost a 12-round unanimous decision. Billy still lives in the Falls and is still active fighting across Canada.

FOOTBALL

1. What Canadian-born quarterback was a Super Bowl MVP?

A. Mark Rypien led his Washington Redskins to a 37–24 win over the unlucky Buffalo Bills (it was their second of four straight Super Bowl losses) on January 26, 1992. Although born in Calgary, Rypien moved to Spokane, Washington, at the age of four. He grew up to excel in many sports and played college ball at Washington State in nearby Pullman, Washington. He turned pro with the Redskins, and, after a few seasons backing up Doug Williams, he found his groove and was twice named to the NFL Pro Bowl team.

2. Who was the first Canadian-born-and-raised NFLer to quarterback his team?

A. Even though Mark Rypien was an NFL starter for years, he left Canada as a young child. Jesse James Palmer, however, was born and raised in Nepean, Ontario. You might say football was in his blood — his dad, Bill, was a pretty good player himself during his six-year CFL career. Leaving home only to play for the Florida State Gators, Jesse was chosen in the fourth round of the 2001 draft by the New York Giants. Playing behind iron man Kerry Collins, Palmer finally got his chance to start on December 14, 2003, against the New

Orleans Saints (he lost, 45–17). In a totally unrelated career move, Palmer's moves were put to the test in 2004 when he appeared with a bevy of single beauties on the ABC-TV series *The Bachelor.*

3. Which Canadian football player shares a name with an NFL star and a certain fruit juice?

A. None other than Whitby, Ontario's O.J. Santiago, who played high school football at St. Michael's College School in Toronto. O.J. went to Kent State University in Ohio, where, under the tutelage of his head coach, the ex-Argo star Jim Corrigall, the six-foot, seven-inch tight end developed into a potential star. Drafted in the third round by the Atlanta Falcons in 1997, in his sophomore year he joined the exclusive club of Canadian Super Bowl participants when his Falcons faced off in a losing effort against the Denver Broncos. After a stay in Cleveland and a one-year stint with Oakland, in April 2004 he signed with the Broncos.

4. Which Canadian quarterback was known as the "King"?

A. Hamilton-born Joe Krol was known as one of the greatest "triple threat" players ever to play in the CFL — meaning he could run, pass and kick with the league's best. He won a total of six Grey Cups (five with the Toronto Argonauts) in a 12-year career that spanned the years 1942–1952 and a return in '55. Along with the Grey Cup victories, he won the Lou Marsh Trophy as Canada's outstanding athlete in 1946 and also was named Canadian male athlete of the year in 1946 and '47. He is a member of both the Canadian Football and Canadian Sports Halls of Fame.

Joe Krol

5. Which Canadian holds the NFL record for most consecutive field goals?

A. Mike Vanderjagt of the Indianapolis Colts owns this mark of distinction. As time ran out in the fourth quarter of a game against the Houston Texans on December 28, 2003, the ever-reliable Vanderjagt booted a 43-yarder that not only broke a 17–17 tie, but an NFL record as well: it was his 41st consecutive field goal. A product of Oakville, Ontario, and a great all-around athlete, Mike went to Michigan State University in hopes of becoming a quarterback, but it was only after he switched to place-kicking and transferred to West Virginia that his college career took off. He broke into the pro ranks in the CFL — where, ironically, he was signed on four different occasions, only to be cut before training camp wrapped up. After a stint in arena football, his prospects improved: he won back-to-back Grey Cups as a Toronto Argonaut before signing as a free agent with Indianapolis, where he has developed into the best and most consistent kicker in the sport.

6. Which NFL team did TSN football analyst Chris Schultz play for?

A. Before he became one of the most knowledgeable and trusted football analysts in the country, Chris enjoyed a successful career as an offensive tackle. At the University of Arizona, he took part in the 1983 Fiesta Bowl and caught the attention of the legendary Dallas Cowboys coach Tom Landry. The Cowboys drafted him in 1983, and he started five games in his rookie year and 21 in total for America's Team before coming home to Canada. A nine-year member of the Toronto Argonauts, Chris was part of the 1991 Grey Cup–winning team. Since retiring from the game, Chris's knowledge and personality have made him a well-respected media figure.

7. Has a U.S. vice-presidential candidate ever played football in the CFL?

A. Yes. Jack Kemp was a young quarterback who, after graduating from Occidental College in California (where he also threw the javelin), appeared in four games for the Pittsburgh Steelers in 1957. After bouncing around for a couple of years, he decided to give the CFL a try in '59. Kemp seemed impressive enough in the preseason, but lost the starter's job to another young American, Joe Kapp. By 1960, he was playing for the Los Angeles (and later San Diego) Chargers of the new American Football League. After a trade to Buffalo, he found real stardom, leading the Bills to a pair of AFL championships and twice being named the league's MVP. He also played in the AFL All-Star Game seven times and helped found the league's players' association. He retired after the 1969 season and was elected a year later to the U.S. House of Representatives; in 1996, presidential candidate Bob Dole named Kemp as his running mate. Kemp's sons have also had careers as pro quarterbacks: Jeff played in the NFL, while Jimmy lasted quite a bit longer in the CFL than his dad, playing for, among other teams, the Argonauts and Edmonton Eskimos.

8. Who made the claim that "It will take an Act of God" to beat the Toronto Argonauts?

A. That boast came from former Argo coach Leo Cahill in 1969. He was referring to the two-game, total-points series his team was playing against the Ottawa Rough Riders. After the Argos won the first game, 22–14, Cahill's bold statement made headlines in virtually every newspaper in the country. Unfortunately for Cahill and the Argos, Ottawa came back to crush them 32–3 to win the series by an aggregate score of 46–25. The Rough Riders then went on to defeat their namesakes from Saskatchewan, 29–11, for the Grey Cup.

9. Which Canadian football legend has played the game, been general manager and president of a CFL team and also served as CFL commissioner?

A. Never let it be said that Jake Gaudaur didn't love the game of Canadian football. Starting in 1940 as a player for the Hamilton Tiger-Cats, the Orillia, Ontario, native started a relationship with the sport that would last more than 40 years. Upon retiring from active play in 1954, he took over the reins as GM, and subsequently president, of the Ticats. During his 14-year tenure in the front office, Hamilton won nine Eastern Conference titles and four Grey Cup championships. After that, Gaudaur, in the capacity of league commissioner, had much to do with making the CFL a strong league that gave Canadians an entertaining alternative to the NFL. He was also one of the driving forces behind the formation of the Canadian Football Hall of Fame.

Jake Gaudaur (right)

10. Who was the first black head coach in the CFL?

A. Former Green Bay Packer and eight-time Pro Bowl-er Willie Wood accomplished that long-overdue feat in 1980, when he assumed the helm of the Toronto Argonauts. Willie, who had quarterbacked the University of Southern California to the 1959 Rose Bowl title, became one of the top defensive backs in the NFL when it was determined that, at five feet, nine inches and 170 pounds, he was too small to play in the league as a quarterback. After retiring, he took to coaching, becoming the first black head coach in pro football with the Philadelphia Bell of the short-lived World Football League. In the late 1970s he came to Toronto to assist his friend and former teammate Forrest Gregg. When Gregg left, Wood was put in charge, and even though he led the troubled team to a record of 6–10 in his rookie campaign, a horrible 0–10 start in 1981 cost him his job. He was replaced by Argos general manager Tommy Hudspeth.

11. Which former CFL star has not only been a pastor but also a very influential U.S. Congressman?

A. There is probably nothing in life that Oklahoma-born J.C. Watts has touched that hasn't turned to gold. He led his Oklahoma Sooners to two consecutive Orange Bowl championships in 1979 and 1980, and on both occasions was chosen MVP of the game. After that, he signed with the Ottawa Rough Riders in 1981, and his strength and athleticism made him one of the top quarterbacks in the CFL. Although the rest of the team unfortunately wasn't up to his level of play, the 5–11 Riders snuck past the heavily favoured Montreal Alouettes to play in the Grey Cup game, where they lost to the powerful Edmonton Eskimos, 26–23. Watts still won honours as offensive player of the game. After retiring in 1986, he returned to Oklahoma, where he became a pastor and won a seat in Congress. Watts is also on the boards of directors of the Boy Scouts and the U.S. Military Academy at West Point.

12. Whose CFL franchise did the league revoke in 2003?

A. Sherwood Schwarz, the owner of the Toronto Argonauts, lost his franchise after encountering financial difficulties and defaulting on the team's payroll. It was reported that Schwarz, a New York insurance magnate, had lost almost $18 million since acquiring the team in December 1999. The CFL ran the club for the rest of the 2003 season, then granted a new franchise to Toronto businessmen Howard Sokolowski and David Cynamon. They have hired Keith Pelley, formerly the head of TSN, as president and CEO of the Argos.

13. Through the 2003 season, how many Heisman Trophy winners have played in the CFL?

A. The 2003 signing of Rashaan Salaam, the 1994 Heisman winner, by the Toronto Argonauts brings the total to six. Billy Vessels, who won the award with Oklahoma in 1952, played in Edmonton and won the first Schenley Award as Canadian football's outstanding player in 1953. After winning the 1962 Heisman with Oregon State, Terry Baker played three seasons for the Los Angeles Rams. He never became a starter, so he tried his luck with Edmonton in 1966, but lasted only one season in the CFL. The 1989 winner, Andre Ware of the University of Houston Cougars, never clicked as a starter with Detroit or Minnesota of the NFL, and played three nondescript seasons in Canada, beginning in 1995. His career highlight was in 1997, when he backed up Doug Flutie with the Grey Cup–winning Toronto Argonauts.

Johnny Rodgers, the 1972 winner from Nebraska, came straight to the CFL from college and was an immediate impact player who, in his five-year career, won a Grey Cup, rookie of the year honours, and a league MVP award. The most successful of all is arguably Doug Flutie, the 1984 winner with Boston College, who came north to the B.C. Lions in 1990 and became one of the most dominant players in CFL history. He led his team to victory in the Grey Cup game three times and was named most outstanding player in the league in six of his eight CFL seasons.

14. Which team has made the most Grey Cup appearances?

A. In 2003, the Edmonton Eskimos appeared in their 23rd Grey Cup game to claim the lead in that category. The Winnipeg Blue Bombers are a close second, having played in the big game a total of 22 times.

15. Who won the 2000 NFL/CFL high school coach of the year award?

A. The NFL/CFL coaching award is one of the highest honours available to coaches in Canada. One of the most important reasons it is held in such high esteem is that the coaches are nominated by their own players. The winner of the 2000 award was Toronto-born Mitch Chuvalo, who, at the time, was football coach at Western Technical and Commercial High School in Toronto. Chuvalo has become one of Canada's most respected coaches and athletic directors in Canada by putting as high a priority on academics as athletic performance. Mitch, who is the son of Canadian boxing legend George Chuvalo, played football for Florida State and the University of Guelph.

16. Who has scored the most points in Grey Cup history?

A. Dave Cutler, the long-time place-kicker for the Edmonton Eskimos, holds the record of points scored in

Grey Cup games with a total of 72. In his career, which lasted from 1969 until 1984, he made a total of nine Grey Cup appearances, winning six times. In 1975 he was selected as the outstanding Canadian in the Grey Cup game.

17. What do ex-CFLers Anthony Davis, Joe Theismann and Raghib Ismail have in common?

A. If you guessed that all three played for the Argos, you're only partially correct. The Canadian Football League has long attracted great athletes from south of the border, especially early in their careers, and the three players named above were highly ranked draft choices who were all runners-up in the Heisman Trophy voting. Others CFLers who can make that claim include Michael Bishop, who played for the Argos; Troy Davis of the Hamilton Tiger-Cats; Tommie Frazier of the Montreal Alouettes; and Toronto's Paul Palmer. That's seven Heisman runners-up who have played in the CFL.

18. Which former CFL star is the most prolific regular-season passer in pro football history?

A. One of the greatest quarterbacks in football history, Warren Moon. If you combine his CFL stats as an Edmonton Eskimo (21,228) with the numbers he posted during an illustrious NFL career, you get 70,553 yards. Second on that list, and tops all-time in the CFL, is Damon Allen, currently with the Toronto Argonauts, with 61,802. In 2003, Allen eclipsed the great Miami Dolphins star Dan Marino, who racked up 61,361 in the NFL.

19. Which TV football commentator won three Grey Cups in his career?

A. Winnipeg-born Chris Walby is the towering bear of a man who co-hosts the CFL telecasts on the CBC. After playing junior football in Winnipeg, Walby got a scholarship to Dickenson University in North Dakota. Soon after being drafted by the Montreal Alouettes in 1981, he was traded to his hometown team in Winnipeg. Along with his three Grey Cup wins, this huge offensive tackle was chosen as a CFL All-Star on nine occasions. He moved into the broadcast booth after retiring in 1996, and he has excelled as a colour commentator.

20. Do you know which team scored the most points in a single CFL game?

A. The Canadian game has always been more wide-open than its NFL counterpart. The wider field and increased emphasis on passing make for a faster-paced game that naturally results in more points being put on the scoreboard. But you have to look way back to October 20, 1956, to find the most explosive one-game performance. On that date, the Montreal Alouettes, led by the great Sam Etcheverry and Hal Patterson (Canada's MVP that season), hammered the Hamilton Tiger-Cats by a score of 82–14. As potent as the Alouettes were, it was, ironically, they who were blown out in the Grey Cup, 50–27, by the Edmonton Eskimos.

21. Which NHL owner was inducted into the Canadian Football Hall of Fame?

A. Harold Ballard, the long-time owner of the Toronto Maple Leafs, was so honoured by the sport of football in 1987. Ballard, who is also a member of the Hockey Hall of Fame, got into the football business when he purchased the Hamilton Tiger-Cats in 1978. As a CFL owner, he was as colourful and as controversial as he was with the Leafs; his battles with Hamilton City Council over concession rights at Ivor Wynne

Stadium were legendary. However, he also did much to restore the Steel City's pride on the gridiron. The high point came in 1986, when Ballard's Ticats defeated the Edmonton Eskimos, 39–15, to win the Grey Cup.

22. Which ex-player and football broadcaster was fired for shooting from the hip on the radio?

A. Mel Profit, the former star tight end for the Toronto Argonauts, was the colour man on Argo broadcasts over radio station CFRB in 1976. He was always known for telling it like it was, and this year was no different, as he criticized the quality of the Argos' performance and their coaching staff. After the 1976 season, the Argonauts delivered an ultimatum to the radio station: if Profit was not removed from the broadcasts, the rights to the games would be assigned to another station. It was at that point that Profit was fired and Peter Martin took his place on the broadcasts. Afterwards, Profit moved to California and today he lives a very quiet lifestyle. The four-time Eastern Conference All-Star was also named by fans to the Argos' all-time dream team.

23. Who was the last Canadian to win the CFL's most valuable player award?

A. You have to go back all the way to 1978, when Hamilton, Ontario's own Tony Gabriel, tight end for the Ottawa Rough Riders, pulled it off. The talented Gabriel was a college all-star when he played for the Syracuse Orangemen, after which he signed on with the hometown Tiger-Cats, with whom he won a Grey Cup in 1972. He was traded to Ottawa in 1974, and he would remain the dominant tight end of his era. He won another Grey Cup, in 1976, and, in addition to the MVP award, he was named most valuable Canadian on four occasions.

24. Who was the only coach to win 100 games in both the CFL and the NFL?

A. Wisconsin-born Bud Grant was a fine multisport athlete who was a collegiate all-star in football, baseball and basketball. In fact, he played two seasons with the Minneapolis Lakers, including 1949–50, when they won the NBA championship. But football was his true calling, and, after playing two seasons with the Philadelphia Eagles, he came north to Winnipeg, where he was a three-time all-star. After retiring, he was hired to coach the Blue Bombers, and won four Grey Cup titles over the next decade. In 1966 he returned to the NFL and led his Minnesota Vikings to four Super Bowl appearances. He won 168 games in the NFL, compared with 122 in the CFL.

25. Who was the only man to coach in the CFL, NFL and AFL?

A. Frank "Pop" Ivy was a great natural athlete who was an All-America as a member of the Oklahoma Sooners. He would then play for the NFL Pittsburgh Steelers and Chicago Cardinals, retiring after the Cards won the championship in 1947. He got into coaching in Oklahoma, where he was an assistant on the squad that won the national collegiate crown in 1950. In '54, he joined the Edmonton Eskimos as head coach and led them to three Grey Cups in only four seasons. In 1958 he returned to the States to coach the NFL's Chicago Cardinals, moving with them to St. Louis in 1960 before joining the AFL's Houston Oilers. He retired in 1984 after a long tenure as an assistant coach and scout for the New York Giants.

26. *The Man Who Lost Himself* is a book about which former CFL star?

A. In 1988, Montreal-born Terry Evanshen was, through no fault of his own, involved in a traffic accident. His head injuries were so severe that he fell into a coma for several weeks, and when he awoke it was discovered that the 44-year-old member of the Canadian Football Hall of Fame had lost nearly all of his memory. The rehabilitation process was very difficult, but he has made progress. The courageous Evanshen now travels across Canada giving motivational presentations about his life.

Evanshen was an outstanding pass receiver who twice won the Schenley Award as most outstanding Canadian during his 14-year career. In 1970, he was a member of the Grey Cup–winning Alouettes, and when he was inducted into the Hall of Fame in 1984, he was the youngest man to earn that honour. In *The Man Who Lost Himself,* the well-known Canadian journalist and human rights activist June Callwood told Evanshen's story.

27. Which B.C. Lions star was known as "Dirty Thirty"?

A. Hamilton, Ontario's own Jim Young got that nickname for his hard-nosed style of play, which earned him the respect of fans, teammates and opponents alike. He played college football at Queen's University in Kingston, Ontario, where, in 1964, he was team MVP. In 1967, the Toronto Argonauts traded his rights to the Lions, and he played 197 games in his career that spanned 13 seasons. He was chosen as the CFL's outstanding Canadian twice, in 1970 and '72. His best season in the league was 1972, when he rushed for 1,362 yards and scored 11 touchdowns. He was elected to the Canadian Football Hall of Fame in 1991.

28. Which CFL quarterback won an incredible five Grey Cups in only six seasons?

A. Warren Moon has been, without a doubt, one of the most dominant quarterbacks ever to have played the game — not only in the CFL but in the NFL as well. After winning the Rose Bowl with his Washington State Cougars in 1978 — he was MVP of the game — he came north and signed with the Edmonton Eskimos, who were on the threshold of a dynasty. In his six-year career (1978–83) he won an incredible five Grey Cups, and in 1983 he earned the Schenley Award as league MVP. His greatness followed him to the NFL, where he was chosen to play in the Pro Bowl nine times and was voted the NFL's man of the year in 1989.

29. Since 1958, when the CFL was officially formed, which city has hosted the most Grey Cup games?

A. Toronto, which hosted the lion's share of Grey Cup games in the years leading up to 1958, has also played host to the most championship games (14) since then. A close second is Vancouver, which has staged the game 12 times. Between them, they account for more than half. The rest, in order: Montreal, 6; Calgary and Edmonton, 3 each; Hamilton, Ottawa, Winnipeg, and Regina, 2 each. Ottawa will move up the list when it hosts the 2004 Grey Cup. The game hasn't been played in Toronto since 1992.

30. Which Canadian two-sport athlete played in a Stanley Cup final and a Grey Cup in the same season?

A. That was Regina's own Gerry James, who played for the Winnipeg Blue Bombers in their 1959 Grey Cup win, then joined the Toronto Maple Leafs, who lost to the Montreal Canadiens in the 1959–60 Stanley Cup finals. A talented all-around athlete, Gerry was the son of Eddie James, who was an all-star football player with the Regina Roughriders in the 1920s and '30s. Gerry went on to win a total of four Grey Cups in his career and was twice the winner of the Schenley Award as outstanding Canadian. He would also one day join his father in being enshrined in the Canadian Football Hall of Fame. He also appeared in 149 regular-season games during his five seasons with the Leafs.

31. What vital role did Greg Fulton play in the operation of the CFL?

A. Greg "Facts" Fulton was known as the league's historian and statistician for 36 years. He also had the thankless task of drawing up the league's schedule for more than three decades, and served as the CFL's secretary-treasurer and as secretary of the CFL players' pension plan. He also sat on the league's rules committee and edited the CFL rulebook as well as its constitution, bylaws and regulations. His connection with Canadian football began in 1950, when he became the official statistician for the Calgary Stampeders.

For his many services to the league, he received the first Commissioner's Award in 1990 and was inducted into the Canadian Football Hall of Fame in 1995. Fulton was also a war hero who was based with the 14th Army Tank Battalion that took part in the ill-starred raid on Dieppe. Canadian football lost one of its treasures when Mr. Fulton passed away in December 2003.

32. Which former CFL star was known as Dr. Death?

A. Dave Fennell was one of the major components in the famed Eskimos dynasty of the late 1970s and early '80s. An Edmonton native, he played college ball at the University of North Dakota, where he came into his own as a fierce competitor and one of the premier defensive tackles in football. Between 1974, when he joined the Eskimos, and 1983, he won an amazing six Grey Cups and was twice named the defensive player of the game. At the 1982 Grey Cup game he was also chosen as outstanding Canadian and in 1979 won the Schenley as the league's top Canadian. He was elected to the Canadian Football Hall of Fame in 1990.

33. Since the modern CFL was formed in 1958, which team has won the most Grey Cups?

A. In the 46 years between 1958 and 2003, the Edmonton Eskimos have come out on top a total of nine times, including five in a row between 1978 and '82. The Winnipeg Blue Bombers are next, with seven, followed by the Hamilton Tiger-Cats, with six. The now-defunct Ottawa Rough Riders hoisted the Grey Cup five times. The Montreal Alouettes are four-time winners (three times for the original franchise, and once since the team was resurrected in 1996). The Toronto Argonauts, Calgary Stampeders and B.C. Lions have each won the Cup four times, while the Saskatchewan Roughriders have a pair of titles to their credit. Finally, the Baltimore Stallions won the Grey Cup in 1995, their second and final season. A year later, they were transplanted to Montreal.

34. Bronco Nagurski was one of two Canadians ever inducted into the Football Hall of Fame in Canton, Ohio. Who was the other?

A. Arnie Weinmeister's name is still mentioned today when old-timers talk about the greatest players in football. This native of Rhein, Saskatchewan, was one of the dominant defensive players of his time and was chosen as an NFL All-Star and Pro Bowl-er four times — which is remarkable when you consider that Weinmeister only played four years in the NFL, all with the New York Giants. (He also played two years with the

New York Yankees of the old All-American Football Conference.) After the 1953 season, he headed north and west to play for the expansion B.C. Lions, who outbid the Giants for his services. It was said that Weinmeister, who stood six-foot-four and weighed 235 pounds, was so fast that at the University of Washington (where he played college football), they would make rookie receivers race him over 100 yards. Legend has it that Weinmeister never lost a race. He was inducted into the Football Hall of Fame in 1984.

35. When was the last time a team won the Grey Cup on its home field?

A. You'll have to go back to 1994, when the hometown B.C. Lions defeated Baltimore's newly formed expansion team, 26–23, at Vancouver's B.C. Place. The game was won on the final play of the game, when Lui Passaglia (who would go on to become the CFL's all-time leading scorer) kicked a 38-yard field goal. Baltimore, coached by the legendary Don Matthews, would only have to wait till the next season to defeat the Calgary Stampeders to become the first and only team from a city outside Canada to win the Cup. (They also had to wait until the next season for their official nickname, the Stallions.)

36. What is college football's Uteck Bowl?

A. The Uteck Bowl is one of the two semifinal games that lead to the championship of Canadian university football, the Vanier Cup. Formerly known as the Churchill Bowl, the Uteck Bowl was renamed to honour former CFL player and four-time All-Star Larry Uteck. After his pro career ended, Uteck became the long-time coach and athletic director of St. Mary's University in Halifax, one of the top football schools in the country. He also served as a city councillor and the deputy mayor of Halifax. Uteck passed away on Christmas Day, 2002, at the age of 50, of Lou Gehrig's disease (amyotrophic lateral sclerosis).

37. What was the highest-scoring game in CFL history?

A. Even fans of the high-scoring CFL would have been shocked on September 1, 1990, when Matt Dunigan led his Toronto Argonauts to victory in a 68–43 barn burner against the B.C. Lions. When it comes to the Grey Cup, the highest-scoring match was in 1989, when Kent Austin and the Saskatchewan Roughriders squeaked past the Hamilton Tiger-Cats, 43–40. Austin was chosen as offensive player of the game.

38. Did Bronko Nagurski ever play Canadian football?

A. The Canadian-born Nagurski was certainly one of the greatest ever to lace up a pair of cleats. He was a world champion in football as well as in professional wrestling. He didn't play in the CFL, but his son, Bronko Jr., played eight seasons with the Hamilton Tiger-Cats between 1959 and 1966. An offensive tackle, the younger Nagurski was named to the Eastern Conference All-Star team in 1962 and '65, and was an all-Canadian in 1962, '64 and '65.

39. Can you match up these ex-CFL players with the movies they had major roles in?

1) Joe Kapp   a) *Rocky*
2) Carl Weathers   b) *The Longest Yard*
3) Lou Ferrigno   c) *Spartacus*
4) Woody Strode   d) *Hercules*

A. The answers are: 1 (b); 2 (a); 3 (d); 4 (c).

Kapp, a Grey Cup winner and all-star quarterback in the CFL and the NFL, played a prison guard known as Walking Boss in the 1974 Burt Reynolds comedy *The Longest Yard*. Weathers played Apollo Creed in the first three films in the Rocky series, as well as the title role in *Action Jackson*. Ferrigno, a former Mr. Universe who was briefly a Toronto Argonaut, was the mighty Hercules. He was better known as TV's Incredible Hulk. Finally, Strode, a former Los Angeles Ram who was a Calgary Stampeder in 1948 and '49, appeared in more than 50 films, including *Spartacus* and *The Man Who Shot Liberty Valance*.

GOLF

1. Has Canada ever won the World Cup of Golf tournament?

A. Yes, and not once, but three times. In 1968, the team of Al Balding and George Knudson were victorious; in 1980 it was Dan Halderson and Jim Nelford; and in '85, Halderson combined with Dave Barr to win the tournament. Incidentally, the World Cup has Canadian roots: the trophy was donated by the Canadian industrialist John Jay Hopkins. The tournament was originally known as the Canada Cup, but it is currently known as the EMC World Cup of Golf.

George Knudson

Al Balding

2. Which Canadian golfer is Hollywood planning to make a movie about?

A. One of the greatest hitters of a golf ball alive: Kitchener, Ontario's own Moe Norman, who is a living legend of Canadian golf. His shyness and discomfort with being outside of Canada kept him from making a splash on the PGA Tour. In recent years, however, he has been giving clinics not only in Canada but throughout the United States. In addition to countless amateur titles, Norman has won at least 40 pro tourneys in his career, including two Canadian senior titles and 11 Florida Winter Tour tourneys.

3. Which Canadian golfer has won two U.S. amateur titles?

A. It was another product of Kitchener, Gary Cowan, in 1966 and again in 1971. One of the best pure players that Canada has ever produced, Cowan won the Canadian amateur championship in 1961 and he has nine Ontario amateur championships to his credit. In '66, he became the first non-American to win the U.S. amateur title in 33 years — since C. Ross Somerville, a fellow Canadian, did it. Cowan survived a stroke in 1997, just as he was to leave for the States for a seniors' tourney. He awoke without the use of one leg and one arm, but only days later the plucky Cowan was out on the course hitting golf balls. Cowan has been lauded by the Royal Canadian Golf Association as Canada's greatest amateur golfer ever.

4. Has a Canadian ever won the Masters tournament?

A. The 2003 season was a banner year for Mike Weir. This native of Brights Grove, Ontario, kicked things off by winning the Nissan Open and was later victorious in the prestigious Bob Hope Classic. But his date with the history books came in between the two. On April 13, 2003, at Georgia's Augusta National Golf Club, Weir defeated Len Mattiace on the first playoff hole after the two had battled to a tie after 72 holes at seven-under-par 281. With the win, Weir became the first Canadian to don the green jacket, joining Bobby Jones, Arnold Palmer, Jack Nicklaus and Tiger Woods in winning one of the four major U.S. pro tournaments — and one that many experts feel is the top golf tournament in the world.

5. Can you name the Canadian golf champion who was a high-level provincial politician?

A. It was the pride of Vulcan, Alberta, R. Keith Alexander. He had quite an impressive resumé, winning both the 1960 Canadian amateur championship and, 32 years later, winning the 1992 Canadian senior title. In between, he competed for and won many provincial and local titles. Elected as a member of the Alberta legislature in 1979, he resigned his seat in 1985 so that Premier Don Getty could have it. He has also served the Alberta Golf Association in an administrative capacity, helping to improve the sport in Canada.

6. Can you name the first Canadian to win a PGA event?

A. You'd have to go back all the way to 1936, when Ottawa-born Kenneth Black's exploits in the Vancouver Golden Jubilee Open became the stuff of legend. The local boy, who was playing in a tough field of international stars that included Byron Nelson of the United States, was far behind at the start of the last round before he roared back to win the event. He was also the 1939 Canadian amateur champion — and was runner-up for that title twice, in 1933 and 1946.

7. Which talented Canadian woman won two U.S. senior titles and was Canada's junior girls', ladies' amateur, and ladies' senior champion?

A. Saskatchewan-born Gayle Hitchens Borthwick won the U.S. senior ladies' championship in 1996 and '99, after winning the Canadian equivalents in 1994 and '95. She won the Canadian junior girls' title in 1961, and followed up a year later with the ladies' amateur crown. A well-respected volunteer and fundraiser, she spent nine years as a director of the

Ada Mackenzie foundation, including two years — 1992–93 — as the foundation's president.

8. It is well known that Lionel Conacher was Canada's athlete of the first half of the 20th century. But who was runner-up for this honour?

A. It was a golfer by the name of Donald Day Carrick. This native of what is now Thunder Bay, Ontario, was the winner of many important local, provincial and national tournaments. The two most important wins of his career were his Canadian amateur championships in 1925 and '27. He also played many exhibitions with some of the greatest golfers of his time, such as the legendary Walter Hagen. Like Conacher, Carrick excelled at many sports. He was an all-star defenceman with the University of Toronto Varsity Blues, and he also boxed, becoming the intercollegiate boxing champ in 1927; he was also Canada's light-heavyweight champion and was fifth at the 1928 Olympics in Amsterdam. He also became a lawyer, and in a move that also paralleled Conacher, went into politics as the federal MP for Toronto's Trinity riding.

9. What did Claude Pattimore achieve in the world of golf?

A. Born in Athens, Ontario, in 1927, Pattimore was just out of his teens when he began working around the province in construction. When he was 21, a demolition blast went off and blinded him for life. Within a couple of years, at the insistence of a friend, he took up blind golf. Only a year later, he was already one of the best blind golfers in Canada. The talented Mr. Pattimore won a total of a dozen Canadian championships, and in 1963 he won the International Blind Golf tournament, earning himself the number 1 ranking in the world.

10. Which Canadian woman golfer qualified for the LPGA Tour on her first attempt?

A. Born in Campbell River, British Columbia, Dawn Coe Jones took up the game of golf in her early teens and was soon winning many local tourneys. She enrolled at Lamar University, where she was chosen as a first team All-American. Since turning pro, she has won the 1992 Kemper Open, the 1994 Health South Palm Beach Classic and the 1995 Chrysler Plymouth Tournament of Champions.

11. What is the oldest golf and country club in North America?

A. The Royal Montreal Golf Club, founded in 1873, has been the site of many golfing firsts. Not only was it the first constituted golf club in North America, but it was the first Canadian golf club granted permission to use the designation "royal" in its name. In 1891, it was reportedly the only club of its kind anywhere to open its doors to women, and in 1904 it was the first to play host to the Canadian Open. Last, but not least, the Royal Montreal was the first club to recruit a professional from England.

12. What did Stan Leonard accomplish in the sport of golf?

A. In his storied 30-year career, he won 44 tournaments, including eight Canadian Professional Golf Association titles. South of the border, he was victorious in the 1957 Greater Greensboro Open, the 1958 Tournament of Champions and the 1960 Western Open.

13. Who did the Canadian Press name as the top golfer of the first half of the 20th century?

A. It was London, Ontario's own Charles "Sandy" Somerville, who was also named Canada's athlete of the year in 1932. Somerville had a long career in golf, one marked by many honours and victories. In 1932, he was the first non-American to win the U.S. amateur championship. He also won the Canadian amateur championship six times between 1926 and 1939. A fine all-around athlete, he also won championships with the Toronto Varsity Blues in hockey (1921–22), football (1921) and golf (1924).

14. How many times have golfers won the Lou Marsh Award as Canada's most outstanding athlete?

A. Four in total. Marlene Stewart Streit was a two-time winner, in 1951 and 1956. A generation later, in 1979, Sandra Post of Oakville, Ontario, received the honour. Finally, in 2003, Mike Weir was presented with the trophy after his scintillating season. Named after the legendary Canadian athlete and *Toronto Star* sportswriter, the award is determined by a panel of sports editors and broadcasters from across the country.

Sandra Post

15. What country has the highest per capita rate of golf participation?

A. You might be surprised to learn that it is Canada. A study by the Royal Canadian Golf Association shows that 19.4 percent of Canadians play golf, compared with only 16 percent in the United States. Nearly five million Canadians hit the links — 68 percent are male, while 32 percent are female. The study also showed that the average household income of golfers is 25 percent higher than the national average.

Hockey

1. **Which one of these great NHL goalies has never won the Vézina Trophy?**

   a) **Ron Hextall**
   b) **Olaf Kolzig**
   c) **Curtis Joseph**
   d) **Jim Carey**

A. If you said Curtis Joseph, you're absolutely correct. One of the top goalies in the league for almost 15 years, it is surprising to note that he has never won the award that goes to the NHL's top goaltender. The closest that this Keswick, Ontario, native has come was in 1998–99, when he was runner-up to Dominik Hasek of the Buffalo Sabres.

2. **Who was the last NHL player to play without a helmet?**

A. The NHL made helmets mandatory during the summer of 1979, but a "grandfather" provision allowed those who were already in the league the option of playing bareheaded. As time went on, helmetless players became rarer. The distinction of being the last to play without headgear fell to London, Ontario's own Craig MacTavish, who retired after the 1996–97 season. The tenacious checker and face-off specialist carved out quite a successful career for himself, winning four Stanley Cups as a player, being appointed captain of the Edmonton Oilers, and going on to become head coach of those same Oilers.

3. Which NHL goaltender has won the Vézina Trophy the most times?

A. Jacques Plante was not only one of the greatest goalies ever to strap on the pads, he was truly one of the most innovative to play the game. Born in 1929 in Shawinigan Falls, Quebec, he broke into the NHL in 1953 and backstopped the Canadiens dynasty of the mid to late '50s. At the time of his retirement after the 1974–75 season, Plante's name had been inscribed on the Vézina an incredible seven times. Coming in a close second, with six, were the incredible Dominik Hasek and another great Canadien of the past, Bill Durnan.

Jacques Plante

4. Did an NHLer ever play every position in one game?

A. Oddly enough, yes. One of the most beloved figures ever to lace on a pair of skates was Francis "King" Clancy. He was born in Ottawa on February 25, 1903, and while he was never physically imposing, he compensated with a fiery enthusiasm for the game that lasted throughout his lengthy career as a player, ref, coach and executive. Turning pro in 1921 with the original Ottawa Senators, he was sold to the Toronto Maple Leafs in 1930–31; he would remain with the team for more than half a century. As a player, he would win the Stanley Cup three times, and one of the more unusual highlights of his career came when he was playing for the Cup. On March 31, 1923, Clancy, who was a defenceman by trade, played all three forward positions and saw action at left and right defence. A slashing penalty was assessed against his Senators teammate, goalie Clint Benedict, and back then, netminders had to serve the time themselves. Clancy was appointed to step between the pipes, and he shut out the Edmonton Eskimos for the duration of the penalty.

5. Who is the most penalized player in NHL history?

A. A native of Weyburn, Saskatchewan, Dave "Tiger" Williams holds the all-time lead in PIM with 3,996. However, his mean streak was combined with a ferocious work ethic that afforded him a very successful 14-year NHL career. Drafted by the Maple Leafs in 1974, the colourful Williams also played for Vancouver, Detroit, Los Angeles and Hartford, scoring a very respectable 241 goals before retiring after the 1987–88 season. Since retiring, he has had a very successful career as a sports entrepreneur.

6. What NHL first can Marguerite Norris take credit for?

A. The Quebec-born daughter of Big Jim Norris, the Detroit Red Wings' boss of bosses, Marguerite was the first woman ever to have her name engraved on the Stanley Cup. She succeeded her father as president of the Red Wings in 1952, and was still serving in that capacity in 1954–55, when Detroit won it all. It would be nearly 35 years before Sonia Scurfield, a co-owner of the 1989 Cup winners, the Calgary Flames, joined Ms. Norris. By 2003, eight women's names had been engraved on the coveted trophy.

7. Who was the first rookie to score 50 goals in the NHL?

A. Chosen in the 1977 junior draft by the New York Islanders, Montreal-born Mike Bossy was, from the onset, one of the most gifted players ever to lace up the skates. In his rookie year of 1977–78 he potted an unprecedented 53 goals. As one of the leaders of the Islanders dynasty of the late 1970s, Bossy was to win four consecutive Stanley Cups. Although his career was cut drastically short by a serious back injury, Bossy retired in 1987 with a total of 573 goals in only 752 regular-season games.

8. Was a player ever named the first, second *and* third star of the same game?

A. It would definitely take one of the greats of the game to pull off that feat, and great is definitely the proper word to describe Maurice "The Rocket" Richard. This superstar extraordinaire put in over 18 years in the NHL, scoring 544 goals and becoming the first player ever to score 50 goals in a single season. But it was on the evening of March 23, 1944, in a playoff game against the rival Toronto Maple Leafs, that the great Richard scored all of his team's goals in a 5–1 win, making him a worthy choice as all three stars of the game.

9. Who was the first goalie credited with scoring a goal in the NHL?

A. Fiery and competitive is probably the best way to sum up the career and spirit of Perth, Ontario's own Billy Smith, who was one of the greatest goalies of his era. Drafted by the Los Angeles Kings in 1970, he was chosen by the New York Islanders in the 1972 expansion draft, and he was to stay there until his retirement after the 1988–89 season, winning four Stanley Cups and the 1983 Conn Smythe Award. Another of Smith's greatest moments occurred on November 28, 1979, when, in a game against the Colorado Rockies, Smith was credited with a goal, becoming the first NHL goalie to accomplish the feat. (He was the last Islander to touch the puck before an errant Colorado pass travelled nearly the length of the ice into the empty net.) Since that time, several others have followed suit; Mika Noronen of Buffalo is the latest, while Ron Hextall and Martin Brodeur have each scored twice in league play.

10. Who was the first Inuk player in the NHL?

A. Even though many Native people have played at the NHL level over the years, it wasn't until October 9, 2003, in a game against the Anaheim Mighty Ducks, that Jordin Tootoo of the Nashville Predators became the first Inuk to play in the big leagues. Born in Churchill, Manitoba, but raised in Rankin Inlet, Nunavut, Tootoo has become a real role model for many young Inuit who have taken up the game. A tough competitor, this five-foot, nine-inch right winger fears no one and has dropped the gloves with just about every willing opponent. Jordin dedicated his rookie season in the NHL to the memory of his older brother Terence, the first-ever Inuk to play professionally, who fatally shot himself in August 2002.

11. Who is the only player to captain two different teams to a Stanley Cup win?

A. One of the greatest ever to play the game (only his former teammate Wayne Gretzky has scored more points), Mark Messier is the very model of the modern team captain. Born in Edmonton in 1961, he was an integral part of the Oilers dynasty of the 1980s, and he wore the "C" when they won the Cup in 1990. Four years later, Messier was the toast of Manhattan when he captained the New York Rangers to their first championship since 1940. In all, Messier has played on six Cup winners; he has also won the Hart Trophy (the NHL's most valuable player) twice, the Conn Smythe Trophy (playoff MVP) in 1989, and the Lester B. Pearson Award (the league MVP as chosen by NHL players) on two occasions.

12. Who is the longest-serving captain in NHL history?

A. Chosen fourth overall by Detroit in the 1983 NHL draft, Steve Yzerman, who was born in Cranbook, B.C., and raised in Nepean, Ontario, emerged as one of the dominant players of his generation. He has played on three Stanley Cup winners, scored more than 700 regular-season goals and won the Hart Trophy. He was named captain of the Red Wings at the beginning of the 1986–87 season, at the ripe old age of 21, and he has held the job ever since.

13. Which NHL team holds the mark for winning the fewest games in a season (with a minimum 70-game schedule)?

A. That dubious honour belongs to the 1974–75 Washington Capitals. In their inaugural season, they were only able to score a paltry eight victories all year, against 67 losses and five ties. Entrepreneur Abe Pollin seemed to have started off on the right foot when he hired the legendary Milt Schmidt to assemble his team. Unfortunately, even with the acquisition of veteran players like Doug Mohns and Bill Lesuk, and the addition of first-overall draft pick Greg Joly, the Caps just couldn't compete. It wasn't until 1982–83 that Washington posted a winning record.

14. Who holds the record for playing the most consecutive games in the NHL?

A. Brantford, Ontario's Doug Jarvis put together an incredible streak, playing 964 games over 13 seasons with Montreal, Washington and Hartford. The owner of five Stanley Cup rings (four as a player), Jarvis was one of the top checking centres in the game, but was also able to score a respectable 139 regular-season goals in his career. After retiring as a player, Jarvis turned to coaching. He spent 14 years as an assistant with Minnesota and Dallas, and is currently the head coach of the Hamilton Bulldogs, the Canadiens' farm team in the American Hockey League.

15. Which goalie led his team to victory after suffering a heart attack early in the game?

A. On February 9, 1972, veteran NHL netminder Bruce Gamble and his Philadelphia Flyers were in Vancouver to play the Canucks. Early in the match, Gamble starting feeling very ill; but instead of leaving the game, he stayed in the net and backstopped the Flyers to a 3–1 victory. After the game was over, he was examined by doctors, who discovered that Gamble had actually suffered a serious heart attack. Gamble retired immediately, but unfortunately his health problems didn't disappear. He died of another heart attack on December 29, 1982, at the young age of 43.

16. Which player scored goals at even strength, on the power play, shorthanded, on a penalty shot, and on an empty net, all in one NHL game?

A. Such an amazing feat could only be performed by an amazing player, which Mario Lemieux has been all through his career. He has taken home enough silverware to fill a small warehouse: his name appears on the Stanley Cup twice; on the Art Ross Trophy, for the scoring title, six times; on the Pearson Trophy four times; twice each on the Hart and Conn Smythe trophies; and on the Calder (rookie of the year). He has also endured and overcome obstacles that would make a lesser man quit: not only has he battled back injuries for most of his career, but he has also beaten Hodgkin's disease, a form of cancer. In 1993, the league recognized his struggles by awarding him the Bill Masterton Trophy for perseverance, sportsmanship and dedication to hockey. New Year's Eve 1988 must be considered another highlight in his illustrious career. On that night, he scored five goals against the New Jersey Devils, leading his Penguins to an 8–6 victory, and each goal was scored a different way. It's a feat that has never been matched in NHL play.

17. What was the highest-scoring game in NHL history?

A. Actually, we have a tie on this one. For the first, we have to go back more than 80 years to January 10, 1920, when the Montreal Canadiens defeated the Toronto St. Patricks 14–7. Then, on December 11, 1985, the Edmonton Oilers, who symbolized the wide-open, high-scoring hockey of the '80s, outlasted the Chicago Blackhawks in a 12–9 shootout.

18. Since 1926–27, when the NHL gained exclusive control of the Stanley Cup and the Ottawa Senators were

victorious, have Canadian-based teams won the Cup more often than those located in the United States?

A. U.S.–based teams have been closing the gap of late (the 1993 Montreal Canadiens were the last champions from north of the border), but teams representing Canadian cities have won the Stanley Cup 41 times, while Tampa Bay's victory over Calgary in 2004 marked the 37th time a U.S. team won it all.

19. **Where the Stanley Cup is concerned, what do Bob Gainey, Jacques Plante, Ted Kennedy, the 1980–81 New York Islanders the 1971–72 Boston Bruins and the 1962–63 Toronto Maple Leafs have in common?**

A. All of these teams and players have had their names misspelled on the Stanley Cup. For instance, the Islanders' nickname was spelled Ilanders, the Bruins appeared as the Bqstqn Bruins, the Leafs were the Leaes, Ted Kennedy's last name was misspelled as Kennedyy and Bob Gainey of the Montreal Canadiens shows up as Gainy. But the unluckiest of all was the legendary goalie Jacques Plante, whose name was misspelled on five different occasions.

20. **Has an individual's name ever been removed from the Stanley Cup?**

A. Yes. The Edmonton Oilers of the 1980s were one of the greatest dynasties in the history of the sport. Their owner, Peter Pocklington, believed in a hands-on management policy, taking great delight in the successes of his beloved Oilers and thinking of the players as members of his own family. So great was his belief in sharing the credit for success amongst the Oilers "family" that, after they won the Cup in 1984, he had his father Basil's name engraved on the cup. When the league found out and realized that the senior Mr. Pocklington had no direct affiliation with the team, they had his name stricken: today, where his name once appeared, a row of 16 X's covers the name of Basil Pocklington.

21. It's well known that Rocket Richard was the first NHL player to score 50 goals in a season. But who was the first to score *more than* 50?

A. Robert Marvin Hull of Pointe Anne, Ontario, was easily one of the most electrifying players ever to play hockey. The owner of the hardest shot in the sport, the Golden Jet was destined for stardom from the first time he set foot on an NHL rink in 1957. On March 12, 1966, Bobby Hull scored his 51st goal of the season against goalie Cesare Maniago of the New York Rangers. Hull went on to score 54 goals that season. Coincidentally, back in 1961, when Maniago was a rookie with the Leafs, he was also in the net for Bernie Geoffrion's record-tying 50th goal.

22. Who played on the Detroit Red Wings' famed "Production Line"?

A. The Production Line was originally made up of two Saskatchewan lads by the name of Sid Abel and Gordie Howe, along with Ted Lindsay of Renfrew, Ontario. Formed during the 1947–48 season, the unit quickly became one of the dominant lines in the sport and played a large role in the Red Wings' Stanley Cup wins in 1950 and '52. After Abel was traded to Chicago in the summer of 1952, his place at centre was taken by Alex Delvecchio of Fort William, Ontario. Delvecchio fit right in with Howe and Lindsay and helped lead the team to two more Stanley Cups, in 1954 and '55.

Gordie Howe

23. Was the Tim Hortons chain of donut shops really named after the late hockey player?

A. You bet it was. Tim Horton was one of the most valuable defencemen of his generation. Born in Cochrane,
Ontario, he played 22 seasons in the NHL, most of them with
the Toronto Maple Leafs. He won the Stanley Cup on four
occasions and was an NHL All-Star a half-dozen times. After
giving the hamburger business a try, Horton was convinced
in 1964 to switch to donuts and, while he continued to play
hockey, started to build a network of franchises. When Tim
died in a car accident on February 21, 1974, Tim's partner

Ron Joyce played a big role in developing the company into an industry leader with more than 2,000 shops.

Tim Horton

24. Who won the Norris Trophy more frequently in his career: Doug Harvey or Ray Bourque?

Doug Harvey

A. Of the two Montreal-born blueliners, Doug Harvey comes out on top. Over his 20-year career, Harvey was chosen as the NHL's best defenceman a total of seven times — second only to Bobby Orr's eight Norris wins. In his 22 seasons with the Boston Bruins and Colorado Avalanche, Bourque won the Norris a total of five times. Harvey won a total of six Stanley Cups in his career and was a 10-time member of the NHL's First All-Star Team. He has been inducted into both the Hockey Hall of Fame and the Canadian Sports Hall of Fame.

25. Has a non-human's name ever appeared on the Stanley Cup?

A. Yes, indeed. The Quebec Bulldogs were one of the pro hockey powerhouses of the first two decades of the twentieth century. Featuring such stars as the great Joe Malone and "Bad" Joe Hall, they won the Stanley Cup twice, in 1912 and 1913. If you look at the Cup, you will find the name Bow Wow engraved on it. The reason for this, or the nature of Mr. Wow's involvement with the team, is lost to history, but rumour has it he was either a mascot or a team member's pet.

26. When was the last all-Canadian Stanley Cup final?

A. At one time it was quite common to see two Canadian-based teams battle for Lord Stanley's silverware. But, alas, times have changed; it's rare enough to see one Canadian city represented in the finals (the 2003–04 Calgary Flames were the first such team since the 1993–94 Vancouver Canucks). The last Stanley Cup final series to pit two Canadian-based teams against each other was in 1989, when the Calgary Flames defeated the Montreal Canadiens, four games to two, to win their first — and to date, only — championship.

27. Match these players real names with their nicknames.

1) Big Bird	a) Johnny McKenzie
2) Pie Face	b) Larry Robinson
3) Spinner	c) Ken Linseman
4) The Rat	d) Brian Spencer

A. The answers are: 1 (b); 2 (a); 3 (d); 4 (c).

28. When was the last Stanley Cup final game of the "Original Six" era played?

A. It was on May 2, 1967. The Toronto Maple Leafs, who boasted 10 future Hall of Famers, defeated their archrivals, the almost equally talented Montreal Canadiens, 3–1 in the sixth and deciding game of the series. The series marked the 13th time in NHL history that a Toronto team (the Leafs, St. Patricks or Arenas) had met the Canadiens in the playoffs, and each side had won six times prior to 1967. It was also the thirteenth Stanley Cup won by a Toronto team since the NHL was formed, and for those who believe in superstition, it was their last to date.

29. What is Guy Charron's unusual claim to fame?

A. Charron enjoyed a solid career as a centre, logging 734 games in the NHL and scoring 221 goals. But what stands out about the Verdun, Quebec, native's big-league tenure is that he never once played in an NHL playoff game. In fact, no other player has gone as long without appearing in the postseason. After retiring, he became a coach, where he was a bit more fortunate, seeing some playoff activity in the early 1990s as an assistant with the Calgary Flames.

30. Which one of these players never won an NHL scoring title?

   a) Bobby Orr
   b) Bernie Geoffrion
   c) Mark Messier
   d) Marcel Dionne

A. The answer is Mark Messier. This shoo-in for the Hockey Hall of Fame, who is currently the second most prolific scorer in NHL history, has accomplished just about everything a player could dream of, including winning six Stanley Cups and the Hart and Conn Smythe trophies. The only title that has eluded him in his 25 NHL seasons is the Art Ross Trophy. The closest he came was in 1989–90, when he placed second to his teammate, the Great One himself, Wayne Gretzky.

31. Can you name the only father-and-son team to win the Hart Trophy?

A. That would be the Golden Jet, Bobby Hull, and his son, the "Golden Brett." The elder Hull, who played 23 seasons of pro hockey, won the award twice, in 1965 and '66. Brett, who followed his dad into the NHL and, like Bobby, became one of the greatest scorers in NHL history, won the honour in 1991. The two Hulls have combined for 1,516 regular-season and playoff goals, easily more than any other family tandem ever to play in the NHL. (Bobby added 346 more in the World Hockey Association.)

Bobby Hull

32. Who made up the NHL's French Connection line?

A. The French Connection was arguably the greatest line in the NHL during the 1970s. The Buffalo Sabres' top unit consisted of three Québécois stars: Gilbert Perreault at centre, Richard Martin at left wing and René Robert on the right. Together for most of the decade, they wreaked havoc on their opponents and led the Sabres to the NHL finals in 1975. Considering that the Buffalo franchise had only been created in 1970, that feat speaks volumes about the French Connection's value to the team. The line was broken up in 1979 when Robert was traded to the Colorado Rockies. Nobody who ever saw them in action will ever forget the gutsy two-way Robert, Richard Martin's slapshot that rivalled the great Bobby Hull's and the electrifying Perreault, who was one of the greats to ever play the game.

33. How many NHL teams did Wayne Gretzky play for?

A. Four in all. When the WHA's Edmonton Oilers joined the NHL in 1979, Gretzky was with them. He led the Oilers dynasty to four Stanley Cup championships before he was traded on August 9, 1988, to the Los Angeles Kings. On February 27, 1996, he was again traded, to the St. Louis Blues, for whom he played 18 regular-season games along with 13 in the playoffs. In July 1996, he signed as a free agent with the New York Rangers, whom he played for until his retirement after the 1999 season. When his career was over he held more than 60 NHL records. To name only a few of his accomplishments, he won the league scoring title 10 times, was a nine-time MVP, and had scored more regular-season goals (894), assists (1,963) and total points (2,857) than any player in NHL history.

34. How long was the longest undefeated streak in NHL history?

A. With such great Canadian players as Bobby Clarke, Bill Barber and Reggie Leach leading the way on the ice and Hamilton's favourite son, Pat Quinn, behind the bench, the 1979–80 Philadelphia Flyers set that record. Beginning on October 14, 1979, when they defeated the Toronto Maple Leafs 4–3, the Flyers could not be beaten until January 7, 1980, when they lost 7–1 to the Minnesota North Stars. Along the way, they won 25 games and tied 10 others, stringing together a 35-game unbeaten streak. It wasn't only the best in hockey history, but in North American professional team sports as well.

35. Why does the name Taro Tsujimoto appear in NHL record books?

A. In 1974, the NHL conducted its amateur draft via a secret telephone conference call, hoping to interfere with efforts by WHA teams to lure top prospects away with lucrative contract offers. The proceedings dragged on, and in the 11th round, Buffalo's front office decided to have some fun. They announced that, with the 183rd pick overall, the Sabres were drafting Taro Tsujimoto, a centreman with the Tokyo Katanas. For weeks, reporters pressed Punch Imlach, the legendary coach and GM of the Sabres, for more details about this draft choice before he finally confessed that it had all been a prank, that Taro's name had been picked out of the phone book and that *katana* was Japanese for "sabre."

36. Which NHL player scored a game-winning overtime goal in the 1964 playoffs?

A. They certainly didn't come any more hard-nosed than Saskatchewan's Bobby Baun. On April 23, 1964, his Toronto Maple Leafs met the Detroit Red Wings in game six of the Stanley Cup finals, trailing Detroit three games to two. The score was tied 3–3 when the great Gordie Howe let loose a shot that nailed Baun right on the ankle. The injury was severe enough that the Leaf defenceman had to be carried off the ice on a stretcher. But Baun, who, instead of going to the hospital, had his ankle frozen, returned to the game and blasted the puck past Red Wings goalie Terry Sawchuk to win the game for the Leafs and force a seventh game to be played. Baun also played in the decisive seventh game, which the Leafs won, 4–0, and only after the game did he go to the hospital, where x-rays showed that he had indeed broken his ankle.

37. Which Canadian province has had the most players inducted into the Hockey Hall of Fame?

A. It should come as no surprise that Ontario makes that claim, with 112. What may surprise you — it surprised me, at least — is that Quebec, with 50, trails by such a wide margin. Prince Edward Island and Nova Scotia, at the other end of the scale, have yet to place anyone into the Hall.

38. Who was the first goalie to wear a mask?

A. Jacques Plante of the Montreal Canadiens is recognized for popularizing the use of the mask, and Clint Benedict of the Montreal Maroons was the first NHL goalie to protect his face, donning a leather mask for a game or two in 1930. But it has become widely accepted that Elizabeth Graham, a goalie with the Queen's University women's team, wore a wire fencing mask in a game in 1927, making her the first known masked goalie.

39. Who was the last goalie not to wear a mask in the NHL?

A. After Jacques Plante reintroduced the facemask to the NHL in November 1959 and improvements to the design and quality of the face protectors were made, goalies slowly jumped on the bandwagon and started wearing them. Throughout the 1960s and into the '70s, fewer and fewer barefaced goalies in the NHL. On April 7, 1974, Andy Brown of the Pittsburgh Penguins, the final holdout, played without a mask in a 6–3 loss to the Atlanta Flames in a game that marked the end of an era. The next season would find Brown in the WHA, playing for the Indianapolis Racers.

40. Which team won the most championships in the WHA?

A. The World Hockey Association, which began operations in 1972, quickly lured NHL superstar Bobby Hull to sign with the Winnipeg Jets and bring the league instant respectability. And it was Hull's Jets who won three Avco Cups: in 1975–76, 1977–78, and the league's final season, 1978–79. The Houston Aeros, led by Gordie Howe, came in second with two titles. The Avco Cup, known officially as the Avco World Championship Trophy, is on display at the Hockey Hall of Fame in Toronto.

41. Who was the first black NHL player to win a scoring title?

A. Jarome Iginla enjoyed a breakout season in 2001–02, when he potted 52 goals and racked up 96 points, leading the league in both categories. Not only did he earn the Art Ross Trophy for the scoring title, but he won the Lester B. Pearson award as the players' choice as MVP. The Edmonton native was drafted 11th overall in 1995 by the Dallas Stars, but was still playing junior hockey for the Kamloops Blazers when his rights were dealt to the Calgary Flames. He has become the team's captain and a cornerstone of the franchise. In addition to the individual laurels he earned in 2001–02, he was an important part of the gold medal–winning Canadian team at the Winter Olympics in Salt Lake City, scoring a pair of goals in the gold-medal game against the United States. In 2004, he led his Flames to a Cinderella season, as they scored upset victories in the first three playoff rounds and took Tampa Bay to the seventh game of the Stanley Cup finals before the Lightning finally prevailed.

42. Which of these players has never won an Olympic gold medal in hockey?

    a) Theo Fleury
    b) Cassie Campbell
    c) Manon Rhéaume
    d) Michael Peca

A. It was truly unfortunate that Manon Rhéaume didn't play for that gold medal–winning Canadian team at the 2002 Winter Games in Salt Lake City. This native of Lac Beauport, Quebec, has been a trailblazer in the sport of women's hockey for her entire career. She played for the silver medal winners at Nagano in 1998, was the first woman to play in a major junior game, and the first woman to sign a professional hockey contract. Of course, no one will forget September 23, 1992, when, as a member of the Tampa Bay Lightning, she faced the St. Louis Blues in a preseason game to become the first woman ever to play in the NHL.

43. How many NHL teams did Bobby Orr play for in his career?

A. Two. The immortal Robert Gordon Orr revolutionized the game of hockey, especially the position of defence, as he proved that a blueliner could be a consistent and potent scoring threat. Born in Parry Sound, Ontario, in 1948, Orr was a sensation even before his rookie year with the Boston Bruins in 1966–67. He won two scoring titles (and he remains the only defenceman in NHL history to have his name engraved on the Art Ross Trophy), was presented with the Hart Trophy three years in a row, and won the Norris Trophy as top defenceman in eight consecutive seasons. On June 24, 1976, he shocked the hockey world by signing as a free agent with the Chicago Blackhawks. Hampered throughout his career by knee problems, he played only 20 games with Chicago before missing the entire 1977–78 season. He returned in '78–79, but managed only six more games before he was forced to retire.

44. Which of the "Original Six" teams has had the most players inducted into the Hockey Hall of Fame?

A. When you include their days as the St. Patricks and Arenas, the Toronto Maple Leafs are winning this race by a nose. Counting the class of 2004 (a trio of defencemen: Raymond Bourque, Paul Coffey and Larry Murphy), 54 Toronto players have been voted into the Hall, compared with 50 Montreal Canadiens. Bringing up the rear are the Chicago Blackhawks: Coffey is the 40th Hawk inductee.

45. Gordie Howe, Guy Lafleur and Mario Lemieux are all honoured members of the Hockey Hall of Fame. What else do they have in common?

A. After being inducted, all three superstars came out of retirement to play in the NHL. Howe, who retired in 1971 and was inducted in '72, signed with the Houston Aeros of the WHA to play alongside his sons, Mark and Marty. He was with the Hartford Whalers when they were admitted to the NHL in 1979, paving the way for the 51-year-old Hall of Famer's return to hockey's elite league. Lafleur, who retired in 1985 and was inducted in 1988, came back that fall to play three more seasons with the New York Rangers and Quebec Nordiques. And Super Mario, who was inducted in 1997, came back in 2000 and helped Canada win its Olympic gold medal in 2002.

46. What hockey legend has been offered the position of governor general of Canada?

A. Born on August 31, 1931, in Trois-Rivières, Quebec, Jean Béliveau was one of the most skilled players in NHL history, and he epitomized dignity both on and off the ice. During his 18-year career with the Montreal Canadiens, he scored a total of 507 goals and 1,219 points and won an incredible 10 Stanley Cups. After retiring in 1971, he stepped easily into the business side of the sport with the Canadiens' front office. When he retired in 1994, he was offered the post of governor general, which, unfortunately, he had to decline due to family obligations.

47. Who is the only female hockey player to score a goal in a professional hockey league?

A. One of Canada's finest athletes, Saskatchewan's Hayley Wickenheiser has broken many boundaries in the world of women's sports. In 2003, she joined the ranks of male professional hockey players when she joined the Salamat team in the Finnish second division. On February 1, she made history when she scored a goal against Titaanit in a 5–4 loss. Wickenheiser, a fine multisport athlete, has represented Canada not only as a member of the 2002 gold medal–winning hockey team but in the sport of softball at the 2000 Sydney Olympics.

48. **What hockey great is related to Lucy Maud Montgomery of *Anne of Green Gables* fame?**

A. Brampton, Ontario's own Cassie Campbell has developed into one of the world's most valuable hockey players. Along with leading Canada to a gold medal at the 2002 Winter Olympics in Salt Lake City, she has helped the national team to five gold medals at the world championships since 1994. And Cassie is related to Montgomery, the author of the classic Anne of Green Gables books. In fact, her aunt and uncle operate the Green Gables museum on Prince Edward Island.

49. **Something very unusual happened in the NHL during the 1966–67 season. Do you know what it was?**

A. Absolutely no trades were finalized during the campaign. I suppose that in this, the last year of the league's "Original Six" era, the coaches and general managers must have been uncommonly satisfied with their rosters.

50. **Who has the record for most points by a goalie in a season?**

A. The winner of five Stanley Cups and a 2003 inductee into hockey's Hall of Fame, Grant Fuhr was certainly one of the greatest goalies to play in his era. This native of Spruce Grove, Alberta, was chosen by Edmonton in the 1981 entry draft. Fuhr quickly became one of the leaders of the high-flying Oilers squad that dominated the NHL in the mid to late 1980s. Always a goalie who liked to play the puck, in 1983–84 he recorded an incredible 14 assists, a record that still stands today.

51. Whose name appears most often on the Stanley Cup?

A. Henri Richard holds the record for most Cup wins as a player, with 11, but it's actually a long-time teammate of his who has seen his name engraved on the Cup the most times. In his 18-year playing career, Jean Béliveau, the former captain of the Montreal Canadiens, was on 10 Stanley Cup champions, one shy of Richard's mark, but after he moved into the executive suite the Habs won another seven times, meaning that Béliveau appears on the Cup a total of 17 times.

52. What do the names Rick Pagnutti, Claude Gauthier and André Veilleux have in common?

A. All three were chosen first overall in the NHL amateur draft. Gauthier was picked in 1964 by the Detroit Red Wings, Veilleux by the Rangers in 1965 and Pagnutti in 1967 by the Los Angeles Kings. The unfortunate twist is that none of the above ever played a single game in the NHL.

53. Which NHL player holds the record for scoring the most goals in a single game?

A. On January 31, 1920, Joe Malone of the Quebec Bulldogs scored seven goals against the Toronto St. Pats. Malone, who was born in Quebec City, was the greatest scorer in the early days of the NHL. He won the scoring title twice, including in the league's inaugural season of 1917–18, when he potted an incredible 44 goals in only 20 games for the Montreal Canadiens. Malone also won two Stanley Cups and is a member of the Hockey Hall of Fame.

54. Can you name the first expansion team to win the Stanley Cup?

A. It was the rough-and-ready Broad Street Bullies, better known as the Philadelphia Flyers. Under the leadership of captain Bobby Clarke, the 1973–74 Flyers were a fitting mix of talent (Clarke, Bill Barber and Rick MacLeish each scored 30 goals) and muscle (Dave "the Hammer" Schultz, Don Saleski and André "Moose" Dupont). Anchoring the team was perhaps the finest goalie of the era, Bernie Parent. After finishing first in the West Division, the Flyers swept Atlanta and edged the New York Rangers to meet Bobby Orr and the Big Bad Bruins in the finals. The Flyers surprised all by taking the series, four games to two. Bernie Parent won the Conn Smythe Trophy, having already claimed the Vézina. Philadelphia repeated as Stanley Cup champions a year later, defeating the Buffalo Sabres.

55. Has a team ever suspended a player for being too fat?

A. In 1949, Maple Leafs owner Conn Smythe decided to make an example of his slightly chubby goalie, Walter "Turk" Broda. According to Smythe, Broda was too heavy to play properly and ordered him to lose seven pounds in five days. The 197-pound Broda had no choice but to embark on a regimen of diet and exercise. The story made the front pages of Canada's major newspapers, and it seemed as if most of the country was following Broda's progress. The end of the five-day stretch coincided with the Leafs' Saturday-night game. Broda stepped onto a scale just hours before game time and weighed in, as directed, at 190 pounds. The new-and-improved Broda suited up that evening, and he proceeded to shut out the New York Rangers.

56. Who was the first junior player to be chosen by the expansion Vancouver Canucks in 1970?

A. Player drafts are often described as a crapshoot, but there was literally an air of gambling to the way Vancouver drafted Dale Tallon. The Canucks were joining the NHL at the same time as the Buffalo Sabres, which raised the question of which team should choose first in the amateur draft. The league set up a wheel of fortune, which would be spun to decide who went first. The Sabres won the spin and chose Gilbert Perreault, who went on to a Hall of Fame career. With the second-overall pick, the Canucks chose Tallon, a talented defenceman from Noranda, Quebec. Even though his career was not as stellar as Perreault's, he put together a solid 10 years in the league and appeared in two All-Star Games. Since retiring, he has worked as a hockey broadcaster and in the front office, and is currently the assistant GM of the Chicago Blackhawks.

57. Which NHL player accumulated the most penalty minutes in one season?

A. Drafted by the Philadelphia Flyers in the fifth round in 1969, Dave Schultz spent three years in the minors before breaking into the Flyers lineup to stay in 1972–73. Used primarily to protect the team's talent, such as Bobby Clarke, Bill Barber and Reggie Leach, Schultz took on all comers and raised havoc wherever he played. In 1974–75, he set a record that still stands today when he racked up 472 penalty minutes. His fights with Boston's Terry O'Reilly and Toronto's Tiger Williams are the stuff of hockey legend. Schultz retired after the 1979–80 season, turning to coaching and serving as commissioner of the Atlantic Coast Hockey League.

58. Which NHL coach was known as Captain Video?

A. Roger Neilson of Peterborough, Ontario, got that nickname for his pioneering work studying and breaking down videotapes of hockey games — a technique that is standard practice amongst today's NHL coaches. After making his name in junior hockey with the Peterborough Petes, he was hired in 1977 by the Toronto Maple Leafs, a post he held until 1979. In all, he coached a total of eight NHL teams, including Buffalo, Vancouver and, in his final gig, the Ottawa Senators, posting a record of 460–381–159. Unfortunately, Roger left us in 2003, after a long and valiant battle with cancer. He is an honoured member of the Hockey Hall of Fame and was named to the Order of Canada.

59. What was the Richard Riot?

A. Maurice Richard was one of the most beloved figures in Quebec's history and a true symbol of francophone pride. Following an ugly melee during a game with the Boston Bruins in March of 1955, the Rocket attacked a linesman. NHL President Clarence Campbell suspended the Canadiens star for the rest of the season — including the playoffs. Not only did the suspension threaten to hurt the Canadiens' Stanley Cup chances, but it would ruin Richard's quest for a scoring title — something he had never won and, as it turned out, he would never achieve. After announcing the suspension, Campbell attended the Canadiens' next home game, on St. Patrick's Day against the Detroit Red Wings. At the end of the first period, with Detroit leading 4–1, all hell broke loose. The crowd inside the

Clarence Campbell

Montreal Forum turned into a mob, throwing eggs, tomatoes and other debris. Then someone set off a smoke bomb, and the game was forfeited to the Red Wings. Campbell got out of the arena safely, but the mob spilled out onto Ste-Catherine Street and caused tens of thousands of dollars in damage. Calm was restored only after Richard went on the radio and pleaded with the rioters to stop.

Bernie "Boom Boom" Geoffrion

60. **Can you match the real name with the nickname of these famous hockey people?**

1) Punch Imlach	a) Francis
2) Toe Blake	b) George
3) King Clancy	c) Bernard
4) Boom Boom	d) Hector

A.

The answers are: 1 (b); 2 (d); 3 (a); 4 (c).

George "Punch" Imlach was twice coach and general manager of the Toronto Maple Leafs, and performed both roles with the Buffalo Sabres. He won four Stanley Cups with the Leafs and took the expansion Sabres to the finals in their fifth year. Hector "Toe" Blake was a great left winger who scored 235 goals in his career, much of which he spent on the same line as Rocket Richard. Francis "King" Clancy did it all in his colourful career. He was an outstanding player, referee, coach, executive and one of the best ambassadors the game ever knew. Bernie "Boom Boom" Geoffrion was one of the first players to use the slapshot as a weapon and was the second player in NHL history to score 50 goals in a season.

Hector "Toe" Blake

61. Why did hockey drop the position of rover from the game?

A. As hockey has evolved, rules have been added or removed to improve the game or make it more exciting to fans. One of the most notable changes was the abolition of the rover. At the turn of the 20th century, teams iced seven players: the goaltender; a "point" and a "cover point," whose roles corresponded roughly to the modern-day defencemen, although they lined up one in front of the other instead of side by side; the three forwards; and, of course, the rover.

Although the rover lined up with the forwards, the position was not strictly defined. A rover was usually the team's most talented skater and puck handler, and would cover the entire ice surface as needed. The others tended to feed the rover the puck for lone rushes on the opponents' goal. As strategy developed and passing plays were devised, the rover position became unnecessary. The NHL's forerunner, the National Hockey Association, abolished it in 1911, and by the 1920s seven-man hockey had disappeared for good. There are currently 19 players who played the rover position in the Hockey Hall of Fame, including Newsy Lalonde, Lester Patrick and Cyclone Taylor.

62. Which team scored the most goals in one NHL season?

A. With such players as Wayne Gretzky, Jari Kurri and Mark Messier leading the way, the high-flying Edmonton Oilers were the greatest offensive force in NHL history during their 1980s heyday. The Oilers of that era own the top five slots on the all-time list, and they reached their peak in 1983–84, when they potted an amazing 446 goals. To put that in perspective, compare Edmonton's output with that of the Detroit Red Wings, who won the Cup in 1997–98. Even with snipers like Steve Yzerman and Brendan Shanahan on the team, they scored only 250 times. The 2000–01 Stanley Cup–winning Colorado Avalanche netted only 270 goals, and they had Joe Sakic, Peter Forsberg and Milan Hejduk.

63. What do Don Cherry, Greg Redquest and Nick Vachon have in common?

A. According to the Legends of Hockey website, they are a part of a select group of 288 players who have played only one game in the NHL. Cherry, a defenceman, made his only NHL stop on March 31, 1955, in a playoff game for Boston, before going on to fame and fortune as a coach and broadcaster. Redquest, a goalie, played 13 minutes for Pittsburgh on March 19, 1978. He became a successful operator of several goalie schools. Montreal native Nick Vachon, the son of long-time NHL goalie Rogie Vachon, spent five years in the minor leagues, broken up by his lone appearance with the New York Islanders in 1996–97.

64. What were the longest suspensions ever handed down by the NHL?

A. Billy Taylor and Don Gallinger were two of the league's finest young players in the mid to late 1940s. Taylor had been a Maple Leaf protégé who, as a child, would entertain the crowds at Maple Leaf Gardens with his skating and shooting skills between periods of Leaf games. Gallinger was a natural scorer who broke in with the Bruins in 1942, at the age of 17, making him one of the youngest ever to play in the NHL. In 1948, Taylor had just been traded to Boston after five years with the Leafs and a short stint in Detroit, while Gallinger, one of the leaders of the team, was in his fifth season as a Bruin. The NHL received information that the two were involved with a Detroit-based gambler named James Tamer and were betting on hockey games. The two were suspended for life in 1948, and the suspensions were not lifted until 1970. Taylor became a scout for the Pittsburgh Penguins, but Gallinger never returned to the game.

65. Can you name the Calder Trophy–winning player who became a player, coach, member of Parliament and broadcaster?

A. Howie Meeker was born in Kitchener, Ontario, and broke in with the Toronto Maple Leafs in 1946–47. He scored 27 goals, including five in one game, and sufficiently impressed voters that he was awarded the Calder Trophy as rookie of the year. Always ambitious, even as he was still playing he ran in a federal by-election in 1951 and won a seat in Parliament. He chose not to run again in the 1953 general election, instead embarking on a new career in coaching. After a stint coaching the Leafs' AHL farm club in Pittsburgh, Conn Smythe called on him to take over the reins in Toronto. After a fifth-place finish he was let go, and he moved to Newfoundland, where he played senior hockey and got into broadcasting. He was a mainstay of the CBC's *Hockey Night in Canada* for more than 20 years.

66. Whose NHL career goal-scoring record did Maurice Richard break in 1952?

A. Montreal-born Nels Stewart turned pro in 1925–26 with the Montreal Maroons, with whom he played for seven seasons before a trade to the Boston Bruins. He retired after the 1939–40 season, having scored 324 regular-season goals, a record that stood for 12 seasons until Maurice Richard scored his 325th on November 8, 1952. Stewart went by the nickname of "Old Poison," a reflection of his love of some of the rougher aspects of the game, which came part and parcel with his natural scoring ability.

67. Which North American all-star team did the Soviets play an eight-game series against in 1974?

A. No sooner had Paul Henderson scored his series-winning goal in the 1972 "Summit Series" between Team Canada and the Soviet Union than the World Hockey Association began play. Two years later, the new league's backers gambled that, if a team made up of the WHA's Canadian all-stars could also defeat the Russians, it would generate even more credibility and fan support. Team Canada '74 included Gordie Howe, Bobby Hull and Gerry Cheevers, none of whom had played in '72, along with Paul Henderson and Frank Mahovlich, who had. Unfortunately, even though the team was very competitive, the Soviet side prevailed with four wins, three ties and one loss.

68. Did the NHL ever play any exhibition games against its rivals in the WHA?

A. It was surprising to find out that both leagues, and their various team owners, would set aside their differences and rivalries and play some exhibition games against each other. Between the autumn of 1974 and the WHA's final season of 1978–79, 67 interleague exhibitions were played. It's intriguing to note that the WHA teams came out on top with 33 wins, 21 losses and 7 ties against the senior circuit.

69. Which NHL player has the distinction of drawing the most penalties in a single game?

A. There are actually two ways to approach this question. In terms of the sheer number of infractions, the winner is Chris Nilan of the Boston Bruins. In a game on March 31, 1991, against the Hartford Whalers he drew an amazing 10 penalties: six minors, two majors, a 10-minute misconduct and a game misconduct. On the other hand, Randy Holt of the Los Angeles Kings holds the record for the most penalty minutes accumulated in one game. On March 11, 1979, against the Philadelphia Flyers, he was sentenced to the sin bin for 67 minutes.

70. The WHA merged with the NHL in 1979. How many teams from the rival league joined the NHL?

A. The WHA was the brainchild of two California entrepreneurs, Dennis Murphy and Gary Davidson. For seven years, their organization was a thorn in the side of the NHL, whose leadership completely underestimated its potential. But by 1979 the WHA was on its last legs financially, and the NHL finally agreed to a merger of sorts. Four teams joined the NHL for the 1979–80 season: the Edmonton Oilers, Winnipeg Jets, New England (soon to be renamed Hartford) Whalers and the Quebec Nordiques. The Birmingham Bulls and Cincinnati Stingers did not make the jump, while the Indianapolis Racers folded before the season's end. It is noteworthy that only one of the four WHA adoptees, the Oilers, have stayed put. The Nordiques moved to Denver in 1995–96, becoming the Colorado Avalanche. Long-suffering fans in Quebec City could only watch as their former team won the Cup in 1996. In 1996–97, the Jets became the Phoenix Coyotes, while a season later, the Whalers moved south of the Mason-Dixon Line, becoming the Carolina Hurricanes.

71. The NHL has seen quite a few teams come and go since its inception almost 90 years ago. Can you match some of these nicknames from long ago with the cities they represented?

1) Tigers	a) St. Louis
2) Eagles	b) Pittsburgh
3) Pirates	c) New York
4) Americans	d) Hamilton

A. The answers are: 1 (d); 2 (a); 3 (b); 4 (c).

The Hamilton Tigers operated for five years, from 1920–21 until 1924–25, after moving from Quebec City. Ironically, the Tigers, who spent four years in the NHL's cellar, finally came in first in 1924–25. Their Stanley Cup hopes were dashed when the players, upset that the schedule had grown from 24 games to 30 without a corresponding pay raise, went on strike.

The St. Louis Eagles only played the 1934–35 season. They were the transplanted Ottawa Senators, whose financial troubles had begun years earlier and forced them to sit out the '31–32 schedule. St. Louis was already home to a powerful minor-league team, and the Eagles couldn't compete.

The Pittsburgh Pirates, founded in 1925, lasted six seasons. Despite the presence of such future Hall of Famers as Lionel Conacher in the lineup, the team's debts mounted, and not even a takeover by a group fronted by boxing champ Benny Leonard could save it. The franchise shifted to Philadelphia for 1931–32 before giving up the ghost completely.

The Americans were New York's first NHL team,

Lionel Conacher

having moved from Hamilton to Madison Square Garden in 1925. Oddly enough, when the NHL grew to ten teams and split into two divisions, Canadian and American, the Americans were placed in the Canadian Division with Toronto, Ottawa, and the two Montreal clubs. The Rangers, who were founded in 1926 and won the Cup in their second season, quickly eclipsed the Americans. In 1941–42, in a last-ditch marketing bid, the team changed its name to the Brooklyn Americans (they still played at MSG) before ceasing operations.

OLYMPICS

1. Which Canadian has won the most medals in the Summer Olympic Games?

A. Dr. Philip Edwards holds that distinction. Born in British Guyana and raised in Montreal, the athletic Dr. Edwards earned his medical degree at McGill University. Over three Olympiads, he earned five bronze medals in track and field. At the 1928 Amsterdam Games, he earned a bronze in the 4x400 relay. Four years later, in Los Angeles, he won three bronze medals in the 800- and 1,500-metre races and the 4x400 relay. In 1936, in Berlin, he took home bronze in the 800-metre race. During World War II, Edwards served Canada with distinction, achieving the rank of captain. The Phil Edwards Memorial Trophy is presented annually to Canada's top track athlete.

2. Who is the most decorated Canadian Winter Olympian?

A. In his illustrious career, speed skater Marc Gagnon of Chicoutimi, Quebec, has won a grand total of five Olympic medals — the same number Dr. Phil Edwards earned in the Summer Games. At Lillehammer in 1994, Marc won the bronze in the 1,000-metre race. Four years later, in Nagano, Japan, he won the gold in the team relay event. Finally, at the Salt Lake Games in 2002, Marc returned with a trio of medals:

a gold in the team relay, another first-place finish in the 500-metre race, and a bronze in the 1,500-metre event. In 2003, Gagnon announced that he was becoming a race car driver when he joined the champion Honda DeSigi team.

3. Who is the only Canadian to earn a medal in both the Summer and Winter Games?

A. Clara Hughes of Winnipeg won a pair of bronze medals for cycling in 1996 at Atlanta, before competing at Salt Lake City in 2002 and taking home the bronze in the 5,000-metre speedskating event. The determined Clara has battled adversity to achieve her goals; she suffered from extreme bursitis, and in 1999 was struck by a car during a cycling training session, only to come back a week later and place seventh at the world championships. Clara also earned a gold and a bronze medal for cycling at the 2002 Commonwealth Games in Manchester, England.

4. How did Canada save the cross-country skiing events at the 1932 Winter Games?

A. In the days leading up to the Games in Lake Placid, the weather was unseasonably warm, creating bare spots on the cross-country course. Organizers were concerned that there might not be enough snow to stage these events, until they came up with the idea of importing snow from Canada. Within hours a convoy of trucks had been arranged, bringing tonnes of snow south of the border and saving the day.

5. Which Canadian athlete had her 2002 bronze medal upgraded to gold because of a doping scandal?

A. At Salt Lake in 2002, Beckie Scott, a cross-country skier who is originally from Vermilion, Alberta, placed third in the five-kilometre free pursuit. It was subsequently discovered that the gold and silver medallists had both been using banned substances. In June 2003, Scott's bronze was upgraded to silver, and in December, nearly two years after the race, she was named the gold medallist — making her the first North American cross-country skier to win Olympic gold. Scott has become a tireless champion of the fight for drug-free sports, and has led a successful campaign for independent drug testing at all World Cup competitions. In her honour, a facility in Invermere, B.C., has been named the Beckie Scott Nordic Centre.

6. Can you match these Canadian Olympic medallists with the year and colour of their medal?

1) **Barbara Wagner and**   a) **1984 silver**
   Robert Paul (skating)   b) **1976 bronze**
2) **Shawn O'Sullivan (boxing)**   c) **1960 gold**
3) **Kathy Kreiner (skiing)**   d) **1976 gold**
4) **Daniel Nestor and**   e) **2000 gold**
   Sebastian Lareau (tennis)
5) **Toller Cranston (skating)**

A. The answers are: 1 (c); 2 (a); 3 (d); 4 (e); 5 (b).

Wagner and Paul won the gold medal in pairs skating at Squaw Valley in 1960. O'Sullivan won the silver in the junior middleweight class in Los Angeles. Kreiner won gold in the giant slalom at Innsbruck. Nestor and Lareau won gold in the men's doubles in Sydney. And Cranston won a bronze in men's figure skating in Innsbruck.

7. What was unusual about Canada's Olympic ice hockey win in 1920?

A. There are a several unusual facts about this, the first Olympic hockey championship. First of all, the Winter Olympics would not exist for another four years, so this tournament was played in conjunction with the Summer Games. To ensure ice would be available, hockey and figure skating were both staged in Antwerp, Belgium, a few months before the actual games started. Canada was represented by the Allan Cup champion Winnipeg Falcons, who breezed to the gold medal, while the United States and Czechoslovakia won silver and bronze, respectively. Finally, there were some significant differences in the rules the teams played by: seven-man hockey was the rule, games consisted of two 20-minute halves, and if a player was injured and couldn't continue, a player from the opposing team was required to sit out to make things even.

8. What sport did Duncan McNaughton win his gold medal in?

A. Born in Cornwall, Ontario, and raised in British Columbia, McNaughton was such a fine athlete that he was offered a scholarship to attend the University of Southern California. It was while studying there that he developed into one North America's finest high jumpers, and he was a last-minute addition to the Canadian track and field team at the 1932 Games in Los Angeles. Because he was based in L.A., he didn't participate in the Olympic trials (travel would have been too difficult). Duncan's gold medal–winning jump of 1.97 metres was a personal best.

9. What crucial advice did Robert Van Osdel give Duncan McNaughton at the 1932 Olympics?

A. Van Osdel, born in Los Angeles, was a great friend and USC teammate of McNaughton's. In the summer of 1932 they were briefly competitors in the high-jump finals. But that didn't dampen their friendship, or Van Osdel's sense of sportsmanship. He told McNaughton, "Get your kick working, and you'll be over" the bar. McNaughton heeded the tip, and successfully cleared the 1.97 metre bar to win the gold medal. Van Osdel, meanwhile, took home the silver. A year later, McNaughton's gold medal was stolen from his car. Van Osdel, by this time a dentist, was again able to help. He made a mould from his own silver medal and made a copy of McNaughton's medal by pouring gold into it.

10. Who was the first black Canadian to win an Olympic medal?

A. Hamilton's own Ray Lewis accomplished that feat when he won a bronze medal in the 4x400 relay at the 1932 Games in Los Angeles. It is a sad fact that Lewis, who worked as a railway porter prior to the Games, encountered racism that prevented him from finding better jobs despite the notoriety of the bronze-medal win. Never bitter and always philosophical, Lewis published his autobiography, *Shadow Running*, in 1999 and was named to the Order of Canada in 2001. Lewis passed away in 2003.

11. What sport does Canadian Jeff Adams excel in?

A. Adams, originally from Brampton, Ontario, has been one of the most dominant wheelchair racers ever to compete at the Paralympic Games. Since his very first win in Atlanta in 1996, Jeff has won a grand total of eight medals — three gold, two silver and three bronze in the three Paralympics that he has competed in. A successful marketing consultant who now makes Toronto his home, Adams has also become one of the most sought-after motivational speakers in the country.

12. Which Olympic gold medal–winning coach has been appointed as the spokesperson for the prestigious Canadian Association of Coaching?

A. Danielle Sauvageau, who coached the women's ice hockey team to its gold medal victory at the 2002 Salt Lake City Games, has been named to this very important position. Sauvageau, who replaced Sharon Miller as the national team's coach, had great success after bringing in a number of new players and implementing a new system for the team. In addition to coaching for many years, Danielle was also a Montreal police officer who spent time on the undercover drug squad.

13. What track event did Robert Kerr win a gold medal in?

A. Born in Ireland but raised from a young age in Canada, Robert Kerr had tasted bitter defeat when he was eliminated from his track events at the 1904 Summer Games in St. Louis. Four years later, in London, he bounced back and won the gold medal in the 200-metre sprint. After retiring, he remained active in sports, working as an Olympic official and helping organize the first-ever Empire Games (now the Commonwealth Games), held in Hamilton, Ontario, in 1930.

14. Who won the 110-metre hurdles at the 1992 Barcelona Olympics?

A. It was Guyana-born and Canadian-raised Mark McKoy who claimed that gold medal. A great all-around athlete, Mark first made headlines at a controversial time. When the Ben Johnson steroid scandal broke at the Seoul Games in 1988, Mark, who was part of the 4x100 relay team, abruptly left Korea shortly before the event. After admitting to the Dubin Inquiry that he had used steroids, McKoy was given a two-year suspension, which he served before returning to competition.

15. What sport did Gerald Ouellette win his Olympic gold medal in?

A. Ouellette was truly one of the greatest all-around riflemen in Canadian history. He won the Canadian championship on three occasions, and in 1956 he won the gold medal in Melbourne, Australia, in his specialty, the small-bore rifle. Tragically, this talented athlete lost his life at the young age of 40 in a plane crash. He is a member of the Canadian Sports Hall of Fame.

16. At which Summer Olympic Games did Canada enjoy its largest medal haul?

A. It was at the 1984 Games in Los Angeles, when, unfortunately, political strife — especially tensions between the U.S. and Soviet Union — prompted the Eastern bloc nations to boycott, much as the Americans and their allies had done four years earlier when the Games were in Moscow. Canada won a total of 44 medals — 10 gold, 18 silver and 16 bronze — in what was by far the most successful Olympic Games ever for Canada's team.

17. Medal-wise, which Winter Olympics was the most successful for Canada?

A. Canadians returned from the 2002 Winter Games at Salt Lake City with a total of 17 medals: seven gold, four silver and six bronze. At the other end of the spectrum, Canada has on five different occasions won only one medal — the most recent instance being at the 1972 Games in Sapporo, Japan. If it weren't for our dominance in ice hockey at some of those early Winter Games, the Canadian contingent would have come home empty-handed.

18. Who was the first woman ever to win a gold medal in pistol shooting?

A. In 1984, Linda Thom of Ottawa was not only the first woman ever to win the gold in this event, but the first Canadian woman to win a gold medal of any description since 1928 and the first Canadian of either gender to win a gold medal since 1968. Thom, who is a member of the Canadian Sports Hall of Fame, was also a director of the Canadian Sports Medicine Advisory Board and vice chairman of the Canadian Advisory of Firearms.

19. Which broadcaster is known as Canada's voice of the Olympics?

A. Born in Winnipeg but now based in Toronto, the CBC's Brian Williams is the consummate professional in his role as anchor of Olympic coverage, a job he has held since the 1984 Los Angeles Games. After working at a number of radio stations in the early 1970s, Williams joined CBLT, the CBC's Toronto affiliate, as a sportscaster before joining the network in 1983. He has twice won the prestigious Foster Hewitt Award for sportscasting, and his fine work has garnered him a total of four Gemini Awards.

20. Who was the Canadian flag bearer at the 2000 Sydney Olympics?

A. It was Caroline Brunet of Lac-Beauport, Quebec. Brunet had been the silver medallist in the 1,500-metre kayak race at the 1996 Atlanta Games, a feat she would duplicate in Sydney. This talented veteran has been a member of the national team for close to two decades. A multiple world champion, she won the Lou Marsh Award in 1999.

21. Which Olympic medallist has been a spokesperson for aboriginal rights?

A. Born in Manitoba but living in Victoria, B.C., the bright and talented Angela Chalmers has not only been one of Canada's finest athletes, but a person of conscience and integrity. She has become a spokesperson for aboriginal empowerment, and in 1995 she received the National Aboriginal Achievement Award. An elite middle-distance runner, Angela won a bronze medal in the 3,000-metre race at the 1992 Summer Olympics in Barcelona. She has also been a gold medallist at both the Commonwealth and Pan American games.

22. At the games in Sydney, the Canadian flag was lowered to half-mast. Why?

A. The flag was lowered in honour of former prime minister Pierre Trudeau, who had passed away on September 28, 2000. A number of Canadian athletes and officials took part in a brief ceremony in the Olympic Village's international zone. Trudeau was a big supporter of sports who played a large role in bringing the 1976 Olympics to Montreal.

23. Can you name the amazing swimmer who has won seven gold medals at two different Paralympic Games?

A. It's none other than Vancouver's own Walter Wu, who has, for the better part of a decade, been one of the top swimmers in the world. At the 1996 Atlanta Games, Walter won five gold medals; at Sydney in 2000, he came away with gold twice, in the 100-metre backstroke and butterfly. Walter was recently inducted into the Terry Fox Hall of Fame.

24. Who won Canada's lone gold medal at the 1952 Helsinki Olympics?

A. It was 17-year-old trapshooter George Genereux of Saskatchewan. George began shooting at the age of 12, and by the time he was 16 he had won three North American championships. George was awarded the Lou Marsh Award in 1952 as Canada's outstanding athlete. After athletics, he studied medicine at McGill University, becoming a leading physician and expert in the field of radiology. He died in 1989.

25. How many times have Canadians won the 100-metre sprint during the Olympics?

A. Even if you don't count the Ben Johnson fiasco of 1988, Canada has had two winners of this prestigious event, which many consider to be indicative of the world's fastest human. The first to win was Vancouver's Percy Williams, who posted a time of 10.8 seconds in 1928 at Amsterdam. The talented athlete also took home the gold that year in the 200-metre race. Sixty-eight years later, Donovan Bailey of Oakville, Ontario, set down all his rivals, covering the 100 metres in a world-record time of 9.84 seconds. Like Williams, the multitalented Bailey took home a second gold medal, in his case as part of the 4x100 relay team.

WATER SPORTS

1. Which Canadian athlete won six gold medals at the 1978 Commonwealth Games?

A. It was only fitting that Edmonton-born Graham Smith would dominate the Commonwealth Games that year. First of all, the Games were being staged in his hometown, and secondly, he was swimming in the pool that was named for his late father, Don. Graham was the first athlete ever to win a total of six gold medals at one Games. It was all part of a great career for a member of Canada's first family of swimming. (Seven members of the Smith family have taken part in international competition.) He was inducted into the Canadian Olympic Hall of Fame in 2002.

2. Has Canada ever won the prestigious America's Cup?

A. In the event's history, which dates back to 1870, no Canadian yacht has ever won, although two have come close. In 1876, *Countess of Dufferin* was runner-up to the American winner, *Madeleine*. The other was in 1881, when *Atalanta* came in second to *Mischief* of the United States.

3. Which sport did Jacob Gaudaur win a world championship in?

Jake Gaudaur

A. Jacob "Jake" Gaudaur of Orillia, Ontario, was one of the greatest oarsmen in the world. The winner of many national races, in 1892 he and his partner, F. Hosmer, won the double sculls championship of the world, defeating the legendary Ned Hanlan and William O'Connor, on Ontario's Lake Couchiching. Four years later, in 1896, the 38-year-old Jake won the singles sculling championship, beating Australia's James Stanvury on the Thames River. He is a member of the Canadian Sports Hall of Fame, and was the father of former CFL commissioner Jake Gaudaur Jr.

4. Which Canadian woman was the youngest swimmer (to date) to cross the English Channel?

A. Marilyn Bell was only 17 when, on July 31, 1955, she made the fabled crossing in 14 hours and 36 minutes.

Bell was the second Canadian woman to achieve the crossing — the first being Winnie Roach, four years earlier in 1951. Bell, who had achieved fame the year before as the first swimmer to conquer Lake Ontario, retired shortly afterwards and had a long career as an educator. Her life has been made into a motion picture by the CBC, and she has been inducted into the Canadian Sports Hall of Fame.

Marilyn Bell

5. Who was known as the "Professor of Swimming"?

A. It must have been preordained that Gus Ryder's life would be interconnected with the sport of swimming. As a young boy, he pulled two drowning teenagers out of Toronto's Grenadier Pond. The driving force behind the legendary Lakeshore Swim Club, Ryder was the coach behind such Canadian marathoners as Cliff Lumsden and Marilyn Bell. A man who touched the lives of many people, he was not only a coach, but also a teacher of handicapped children, an astute businessman and an excellent athlete in his own right. He received the Order of Canada in 1975.

6. What sport would you identify with Vancouver's Howard Firby?

A. Over the course of his lengthy career, Firby has been one of the world's busiest and most successful swimming coaches. He was head coach of the Canadian Olympic team in 1964, and served in the same capacity at the Commonwealth Games in 1958 and '66. Many of his swimmers also took part in the 1955 Pan American Games. His charges, who have won more than 100 national titles and set a dozen world records, have included such stars as Elaine Tanner and Ralph Hutton. His teams won national team titles from 1961 until 1967 inclusive. Firby also founded the Canadian Swimming Coaches Association and the Canadian Dolphins Swim Club, and he has been inducted into both the Canadian Sports and the International Swimmers Halls of Fame.

7. Which current Canadian swimming champion has held four world records?

A. A true role model and an elite athlete, Winnipeg's Kirby Côté is one of the top handicapped swimmers in the world today. She joined the Winnipeg Wave Swim Club and an athletic career was born. Since making the national team in 2000, she has not only won two gold medals at the 2000 Sydney Paralympics, she has set world records in the 100- and 200-metre breaststroke, the 200-metre individual medley and the 800-metre freestyle. She is a favourite to return from the 2004 Games in Athens with medals.

8. Beth Leboff of Montreal was the first Canadian to win a world title in what sport?

A. In 1992 in Thurrock, England, Leboff placed first in the women's jump event at the World Barefoot Water-Ski Championships. Water-skiing from a young age, she took up barefoot skiing at the urging of friends and proved to be a natural at the sport. The winner of the 1991 Canadian slalom title, the following year Beth won the national overall championship. She then set her sights on an academic career and is now a practising attorney in Florida.

9. Which Canadian diving champion was a famous model and Hollywood stuntman?

A. Born in 1919 on a farm just outside of Winnipeg, Russ Saunders was a natural multisport athlete who at one time had thoughts of becoming a professional acrobat. A natural diver, he won many local and provincial titles, and then in 1939 won the national championship. It was at that point that the colour-blind Saunders was rejected by the Royal Canadian Air Force and packed his bags to Hollywood, where he found fame and fortune. He was the regular double for Gene Kelly, and was Alan Ladd's double in the gunfight and fighting scenes in the movie *Shane*. In 1950, he was chosen by the artist Salvador Dali to be the model in the painting *Christ of St. John of the Cross.*

10. Which Canadian was selected as the NCAA's woman diver of the year?

A. Born in Edmonton and raised in North Vancouver, Blythe Hartley has made quite a name for herself south of the border. As the leader of the USC Trojans women's dive team, she has never finished lower than third in any event and has won four Pac-10 titles. But the highlight of this young lady's career to date occurred in 2001 in Fukuoka, Japan, when she won the world championship in the one-metre springboard. She is an incredible 16-time Canadian national champion (in different age groups) and was selected as Junior Female Athlete of the Year at the Canadian Sports Awards in 1999.

11. Which famous Canadian swimmer was known as "Mighty Mouse"?

A. One of the most successful Canadian swimmers ever, Elaine Tanner was nicknamed Mighty Mouse for her small four-foot 10-inch stature. Born in Vancouver, she realized that she wanted to win a gold medal after watching the swimming finals at the 1960 Rome Olympics. She won many local and national titles, and in 1966, at the age of 15, she took a prominent place on the international stage when she won four gold medals and three silvers at the 1966 Commonwealth Games. That year, she was also selected as Canada's outstanding athlete. She won two silver medals at the 1968 Olympics in Mexico City and retired soon afterward at the age of 18. She was inducted into the Canadian Sports Hall of Fame in 1971, and since 1972 the Elaine Tanner Award is presented to Canada's top junior female athlete.

12. What sport was June Taylor a champion in?

A. She was one of the pioneers in the popularization of synchronized swimming. A graduate of the University of Western Ontario, she won four Canadian championships in the fledgling sport during the early 1950s. Oddly enough, over the same period she was also named several times as the U.S. champion. She travelled extensively throughout the United States, promoting the sport and giving demonstrations. She retired in 1955.

13. Who was the youngest swimmer to cross Lake Ontario?

A. Jocelyn Muir was 15 in September 1981, when she set out to complete the 32-mile swim across the cold lake. She was accompanied by her coaches, Joan and Bill Lumsden, who were both there when Marilyn Bell made her historic swim in 1954. The following year, in Atlantic City, she won the women's world championship. Conquering Lake Ontario once again would be next on the young lady's list of accomplishments, but this time she would swim *around* the lake — a 521-nautical-mile test of endurance. Swimming in support of multiple sclerosis research, she swam seven miles a day, six days a week, and completed the circuit in 60 days. She was the first to swim around the lake, and her swim was the longest international marathon ever. She is currently a swimming coach in New Jersey.

14. What sport did Judy McClintock-Messer win a world title in?

A. Judy was one of the biggest names in the world of waterskiing for over 20 years. Born in Mississauga, Ontario, she won several national titles throughout the 1980s. In 1991, her strong performance helped lead the Canadian water-ski team to break the Americans' 40-year-old stranglehold on the world championship. On September 17, 1995, Judy realized a lifelong dream when she won the overall women's world championship. She is currently involved in the fitness industry in the United States.

15. What invention by a Canadian journalist is used in the sport of sailing?

A. A former reporter and editor of the now-defunct Montreal *Star*, Bruce Kirby moved stateside to work for a sailing publication. In the 1960s he began designing sailboats, and in 1969 he designed the Laser, which would become the most successful boat of its class. The sailboat, which is almost 14 feet long, went into production in Quebec in 1971, has gained Olympic status, and more than a quarter-million have reportedly been sold.

16. Which Canadian swimmer won a gold medal at the 1973 world championships?

A. Bruce Robertson achieved this milestone by winning the 100-metre butterfly event in 1973. A member of the Canadian Dolphins Swim Club, Robertson also won a silver and bronze medal at the 1972 Summer Games in Munich. Also a gold medallist at the 1974 Commonwealth Games, Robertson has held more than 30 individual and relay Canadian titles in his illustrious career. He was appointed as an Officer of the Order of Canada and in 1977 was inducted into the Canadian Sports Hall of Fame.

WINTER SPORTS

1. Who was the first Canadian to win a world championship in skiing?

A. Born in Montreal, Lucille Wheeler started skiing at the tender age of two, and by the time she was 12 she had already won her first Canadian championship. Selected to the national team at the age of 14, she began to make a name for herself on the international scene. In 1956, she won a bronze medal in downhill at the Winter Olympics in Cortina d'Ampezzo, Italy, becoming the first Canadian to ever win an Olympic ski medal. Two years later, in Austria, Lucille took the FIS world championship in the downhill and giant slalom to become the first Canadian champ ever. She went on that year to win the Lou Marsh Trophy as Canada's outstanding athlete. She is also a member of the Canadian Sports Hall of Fame.

2. Which Canadian figure skater has won the most Canadian women's championships?

A. One of the dominant women figure skaters of the 1920s and 1930s, Toronto's Constance Samuel won a total of nine Canadian titles in her illustrious career. She also won a total of three North American championships. This highly talented member of the Toronto Skating Club represented

Canada at the 1932 Lake Placid Olympics, where she fell just short of a medal, placing fourth.

3. Who won more Canadian titles in her career: Elizabeth Manley or Jennifer Robinson?

A. It is Barrie, Ontario's own Jennifer Robinson who comes out on top on this score. Jennifer, who announced her retirement from competition in March 2004, has won a total of six Canadian women's titles in her career. Known for her elegant grace on and off the ice, she also placed seventh at the 2002 Winter Olympics in Salt Lake City. Elizabeth Manley, who was the darling of Canadian skating throughout the 1980s, won a total of three Canadian championships to go along with her silver medal at the 1988 Winter Games in Calgary.

4. Which Canadian was the youngest downhill skier to win a World Cup event?

Ken Read

A. It was the unofficial leader of the Crazy Canucks, Calgary's Ken Read. On December 7, 1975, the 19-year-old accomplished the feat by winning the event at Val d'Isère, France. Read would win a total of five World Cup events in his career, along with seven national championships. He was presented with the Lou Marsh Award in 1979 and was inducted into the Canadian Sports Hall of Fame in 1986. In May of 2002, Read was hired as the president of Alpine Canada, the first world-class athlete to hold the position.

5. Which ice sport was invented by a Canadian by the name of Sam Jacks?

A. It isn't common knowledge, but James Naismith isn't the only Canadian to have invented a popular sport. Even though it will probably never get to be a fraction as popular as basketball, for hundreds of thousands of girls around the world who play it, ringette will do just fine. Sam Jacks was the director of parks and recreation in the city of North Bay, Ontario. He saw a need for a winter sport that would keep girls busy in the cold months, so he invented, and put to paper the rules and designs of, ringette. After presenting it to the local government, they assigned a gentleman by the name of Red McCarthy the task of putting the game to practical use. The first game of ringette took place in 1963, in Espanola, Ontario.

6. How many Canadian figure skaters have won the Lou Marsh Award as Canada's outstanding athlete?

A. From Barbara Ann Scott, who won the award three times, to Jamie Salé and David Pelletier, figure skaters have been well represented in the winner's circle of this respected award, winning a total of eight times. The winners, in chronological order, are: Scott (1945, '47 and '48), Barbara Wagner and Bob Paul (1959), Don Jackson (1962), Petra Burka (1965), Kurt Browning (1990), and Salé and Pelletier (2001).

7. How many times has Emanuel Sandhu won the Canadian men's figure skating championship?

A. The Toronto-born Sandhu has won three Canadian men's titles, in 2001, '03 and '04. Sandhu began skating at the age of eight and has been earning awards and accolades ever since. He had a very strong eighth-place finish at the 2004 world championships and won the highly regarded 2004 ISU Grand Prix of Figure Skating, where he edged out the current world champ, Evgeni Plushenko.

8. Which Canadians won the world ice dance title in 2003?

A. Shae-Lynn Bourne and Victor Kraatz have been on the wrong end of some very questionable judging over the past decade. The 10-time Canadian champions just couldn't get a break from the international judges who didn't know how to interpret their routines, especially their lively and athletic "Riverdance" number. That all changed on March 28, 2003, in Washington, D.C., when they finally became the first Canadians ever to win the ice dance title. After winning, these partners of 13 years announced their retirement from amateur skating.

9. Which Canadian pair won both the gold and silver medals at the 2002 Winter Olympics?

A. It was one of the most controversial incidents in sports history when the uproar over the pairs skating judging erupted at the 2002 Salt Lake City Olympics. Canadians Jamie Salé and David Pelletier had clearly been the best team on the ice, but the gold medal was awarded to the Russian team of Yelena Berezhnaya and Anton Sikharulidze. Salé and Pelletier were awarded the silver. After the media began to report on the injustice, an investigation was opened and the French judge admitted that her vote had been influenced. It was then that the International Olympic Committee overturned the decision, and the Canadians were awarded a second set of medals and crowned as co-winners of Olympic gold. They have since turned professional and are touring in ice shows.

10. Who was the first Canadian woman figure skater to compete in the Winter Olympics?

A. At the very first Olympics, held in Chamonix, France, in 1924, Canada was represented by a pretty 15-year-old girl by the name of Cecil Smith Hedstrom. Participating in both the singles and pairs competitions, it was a growing experience for her. After winning the Canadian senior women's title in 1925 and '26, she became the first Canadian to attain the prestigious Gold Medal Test. At the St-Moritz games in 1928, she skated to a fifth-place finish. The high point of her career came in 1930, when she finished second to the legendary Sonja Henie at the world championships.

11. Did the pairs team of Isabelle Brasseur and Lloyd Eisler ever win a world championship?

A. Brasseur, from St-Jean-sur-Richelieu, Quebec, and Eisler, of Seaforth, Ontario, won their one and only world title in 1993. These five-time Canadian pairs champions also had the great skill to land in the medals at the world championships on five occasions.

Lloyd Eisler and Isabelle Brasseur

12. Who was nicknamed the "Tiger of the Slopes"?

Nancy Greene

A. It was none other than B.C. native Nancy Greene. A member of the national ski team from 1959 until 1968, she was the gold medallist in the giant slalom and won silver in the slalom at the 1968 Olympics in Grenoble, France. She retired shortly after the Games. Named Canada's female athlete of the year in 1967, she was won the Lou Marsh Trophy twice, in 1967 and again in '68. Greene was also a pacesetter in the world of commercial endorsement, helping popularize Mars bars to a generation of consumers.

13. Which skier won a World Cup event with a broken wrist?

A. All through her career, Kate Pace-Lindsay of North Bay, Ontario, always exhibited great determination and courage. And never were these qualities more on display than in

1993, at Morioko-Shizukuishi. When the world champion sprinter Donovan Bailey was asked to name the most impressive athlete he had ever met, his answer was Kate Pace-Lindsay. In 2001, this four-time Canadian champion was named to the Honour Roll of Canadian Skiing, the most prestigious award for Canadian skiers. She also works as a colour commentator for CTV Sports.

14. Which Canadian skating pair was the first to win a world championship?

A. Francis Dafoe and Norris Bowden were the first to start a tradition that would see Canadian skaters become one of the dominant forces in the world in pairs skating. In Paris on February 10, 1954, the four-time Canadian champions achieved a Canadian first when they won the world pairs skating championship, a feat they would duplicate the following year. Then, in 1956, they won a silver medal at the Winter Olympics in Cortina d'Ampezzo. After retiring, they both became international judges and both have kept their hands in the sport.

15. Which Canadian speed skating champion was also a top cyclist?

A. Winnipeg's Sylvia Burka was a five-time Canadian champion who also won world titles in 1976 and '77. A great all-around athlete, she took up cycling, and within a few years she had broken several indoor cycling records. One of the greatest of Canadian athletes, she has been chosen as Manitoba's athlete of the year on five occasions. In the year 2000, she was chosen as Manitoba's female athlete of the century and was inducted into the Canadian Sports Hall of Fame. Her speed-skating success brought Canada to the foreground in the sport and opened doors for such Canadian stars as Cindy Klassen, Susan Auch and Catriona le May Doan.

16. What was Armand Bombardier's contribution to winter recreation and sport?

A. Bombardier, who hailed from Valcourt, Quebec, was a man who showed mechanical aptitude from a very young age. With money that he had borrowed from his family, he opened his first garage at the age of 19. He was always experimenting, trying to build modified vehicles that would make travel more practical for small villages during the harsh winter months. In the winter of 1934, tragedy befell the Bombardier family when Armand's two-year-old son died of peritonitis before they could get him to a hospital. It was after that tragedy that Armand went straight to work on the invention that would revolutionize winter transport; by 1936, he had built the first working prototype of a snowmobile. Canadian winters would never be the same.

17. Who is the only Canadian ever to win the world speed skating championship?

A. You have to go back more than a century, to the year 1897, when Winnipeg-born Jack McCulloch arrived in Montreal for the world championships. By the time the event was over, Jack had won the 1,000-, 1,500-, and 5,000-metre events outright and placed second in the 500-metre race. Along with his world title, he was also crowned Canada's national champ twice, in 1893 and 1897. A fine all-around athlete, he also played hockey for the Winnipeg Victorias and was ranked as a cyclist and rower.

18. Did Brian Orser ever win a world figure skating championship?

A. Born in Penetang, Ontario, Brian was an eight-time Canadian champion whose artistry and imaginative routines made him one of the finest skaters of his time. Fans will never forget the on-ice rivalry between Orser and the American Brian Boitano, which produced some of the finest suspense and excitement in the sport. At the 1987 world championships, held in Cincinnati, Ohio, Orser edged out Boitano to win his one and only world title. Since retiring from amateur competition, Orser has had a very successful career as a professional skater and in touring ice shows.

Brian Orser

WRESTLING

1. Who is Larry Shreeve better known as?

A. Don't be fooled by his mild-sounding name. Shreeve is arguably the most vicious and unpredictable man ever to enter a pro wrestling ring: Abdullah the Butcher. Even though he was billed as the "Madman from the Sudan," the Butcher was actually born in 1936 in Windsor, Ontario, making this master of mat mayhem one of Canada's favourite sons. One of the sport's great draws for more than 40 years, his feuds with such stars as the Sheik and André the Giant are legendary. Always in great demand, he has headlined cards in virtually every major city in the world where wrestling is presented. Now semi-retired, you can visit Larry at his very popular Abdullah the Butcher House of Ribs and Chinese Food in Atlanta, Georgia.

2. Which great Canadian wrestling icon entered this world as William Potts?

A. Until the emergence of Bret Hart on the world scene in the 1980s, none represented Canada in a more positive light than the great Whipper Billy Watson. Born in East York (now part of the city of Toronto) in 1915, the athletic Potts went to England in his early 20s and there, at the urging of his friends, he decided to give wrestling a serious try. A natural from the outset, he honed his skills in the U.K. for a few years before returning to Canada, where he soon became a star of the sport. His career hit its peak in 1947, when he defeated Wild Bill Longson. Another highlight was in 1956, when he pinned the legendary Lou Thesz for a second reign as world champ. A kindly gentleman outside the ring, he was the driving force in raising millions of dollars for the Easter Seals and was a hero to millions for his philanthropic work in aid of needy children. A recipient of the Order of Canada, this proud Canadian passed away of a heart attack in 1990, at the age of 75.

3. What did Whipper Watson, Gene Kiniski, Chris Benoit and Ronnie Garvin have in common?

A. Along with being proud Canadians, the members of this rough and tough foursome (along with many others) were all crowned world champion in their storied careers. It is an incredible fact that Canadians develop a disproportionately large number of successful international wrestling stars. From such stars as Yvon Robert and Whipper Watson in the 1940s and '50s to such current stars as Benoit, Chris Jericho and Trish Stratus, Canadians have definitely achieved monumental successes inside the squared circle.

4. What connection does former NHLer Ted Irvine have with professional wrestling?

A. Born in Winnipeg, Ted Irvine was a scrappy left winger who was able to put together a very respectable 10-year career in the NHL, scoring 154 goals for the Los Angeles Kings, New York Rangers and St. Louis Blues. During that period, he also had a huge hand in bringing his son Christopher into the world. Little did he know then that the younger Irvine would grow up to become the cocky, strutting Chris Jericho, one of the biggest stars in the world of professional wrestling. This multiple world champion has always been proud and vocal about his Canadian roots; similarly, his father, now a financial planner in Winnipeg, has made no bones about how proud he is of his champion son.

5. Which famous Canadian wrestling legend was known to all as the Killer?

A. One of the all-time great villains in the world of wrestling, big Wladek Kowalski was born in Windsor, Ontario, the son of hard-working Polish immigrants. The huge (six feet, six inches) Kowalski was a natural athlete who, due to his size and aggressiveness, was a natural for the world of professional wrestling. Over a career that spanned nearly 30 years, Kowalski took part in an estimated 6,000 matches. The many highlights of this legend's career include taking part in the very first televised match in Canada in 1953 and, of course, the legendary 1954 match in which he inadvertently tore off the ear of the legendary Yukon Eric. Kowalski, who until recently ran a very successful wrestling school in Boston, has been instrumental in discovering such great wrestling talent as Chyna (Joanie Laurer) and WWE superstar Hunter Hearst Helmsley.

6. Was André the Giant Canadian?

A. Not quite, but the huge (seven-foot, four-inch) Frenchman never hid his love for the country that opened many doors for his career. He was born André Rousimoff in Grenoble, and he landed in Montreal in the early 1970s to make his North American debut as a professional wrestler. Billed as Jean Ferré, he took the wrestling world by storm. He loved Montreal, so he made it his base of operations for a number of years, even opening a restaurant there and becoming a partner in the local wrestling promotion outfit.

André was for years one of the most sought after and popular athletes in the world. The much-travelled giant truly became a citizen of the world, but one who never forgot how much Canada meant to him.

7. Mix and match the real and professional names of these current wrestling stars.

1) Val Venis	a) Jason Reso
2) Test	b) Adam Copeland
3) Edge	c) Andrew Martin
4) Christian	d) Sean Morley

A. The answers are: 1 (d); 2 (c); 3 (b); 4 (a).

8. Which Canadian legend was both an NFL Hall of Famer *and* a world champion wrestler?

A. These days, adjectives like "great" or "legendary" are used so liberally and with such ease to describe any athlete who happens to rise above the average. What, then, would you call an athlete who was named to the 1929 All-America team at two positions (fullback and tackle) and received votes at a third (end), a member of — and driving force behind — three NFL championship teams with the Chicago Bears, and a two-time world wrestling champion? You would call him Bronko Nagurski.

Born in Rainy River, Ontario, Nagurski is still known as one of the greatest athletes to compete in any sport. After helping the Bears to back-to-back NFL titles in 1932 and '33, Nagurski trained his sights on the wrestling world, where, in 1939, he defeated the infamous Lou Thesz for the NWA world championship. After losing the belt, he won it back in 1941. When the Second World War left the Bears shorthanded, Bronko returned to football and helped Chicago to another championship. He retired from the mat wars in 1960 to run a service station in International Falls, Minnesota, where he passed away in 1990.

9. Did a professional wrestler ever make it to high politics here in Canada?

A. Jesse "The Body" Ventura made waves in 1998 when he was elected governor of Minnesota, but he's not the only pro wrestler to enter public service after the end of his mat career. Amongst his many sporting careers, Toronto's own Lionel "The Big Train" Conacher — Canada's athlete of the first half of the 20th century and a member of the Canadian Sports Hall of Fame as well as halls of fame dedicated to football, hockey and lacrosse — had a brief but successful turn inside the squared circle. In November 1931, while he was still playing for the NHL's Montreal Maroons, he signed a contract with Toronto promoter Ivan Michailoff and took part in a couple dozen bouts during the summer of '32, reportedly going undefeated. In the fall of 1932 he was back on the ice with the Maroons. After retiring his trunks — and all of his other sports gear — in 1937, Conacher began a successful political career, winning a by-election that gave him a seat in the Ontario legislature. In 1949, he was elected to the federal Parliament, winning re-election in 1953. During the annual softball game between members of Parliament and the press gallery in 1954, Conacher was legging out a triple when he collapsed, having suffered a fatal heart attack.

10. Which multiple winner of the world championship belt was born Trisha Stratigias in Toronto?

A. This beautiful, ambitious ball of fire, better known to her vast legion of fans as Trish Stratus, was born in Toronto on December 18, 1975. Never mistake her for a dumb blonde: before she embarked on her wrestling career, Trish was a very serious student who took biology and kinesiology at York University in hopes of entering medical school. Always a natural athlete, she parlayed her impressive physique and beauty into a successful career as a fitness model; her image has graced the covers of many magazines. She then convinced the honchos at the WWE that she was a natural for their sports entertainment business. Since her debut in 2000, Trish has won the women's title numerous times and has truly become the top diva in the sport of professional wrestling.

11. Which Canadian wrestling superstar was known for his excellence of execution?

A. I can bet you that if you were to go anywhere in our great country, you'd be hard pressed to find anyone who didn't recognize the name Bret "The Hitman" Hart. Bret turned pro in Calgary under the watchful eye of family patriarch and wrestling legend Stu Hart. When he went to work for Vince McMahon and the WWF, his career skyrocketed. Teamed with his brother-in-law, Jim "The Anvil" Neidhart, he was a two-time winner of the world tag-team championship belt, and he claimed the solo title on five different occasions. Hart suffered a career-ending concussion in 1999, as well as a stroke in 2002, but since retiring has made a name for himself as an entrepreneur and columnist for the *Calgary Sun*.

12. Was Yvon Robert ever a world wrestling champion?

A. You bet he was. He was as much a hero to French-Canadian wrestling fans as his friend and frequent tag-team partner Whipper Billy Watson was to anglophones. In his native Montreal on October 7, 1942, Robert defeated Bill

Longson for the coveted NWA world championship. It was said that Robert was such a popular figure in Quebec that, in a poll taken in the 1950s, he beat out hockey legend Maurice Richard as the province's most popular athlete. At one time he was even counted seriously as a potential candidate for mayor of Montreal. After nearly 30 years in the business, he had to give it up due to serious health problems. This proud Canadian and Quebecer left us in 1971 at the age of 56.

13. Who was Lionel Giroux better known as?

A. It would be next to impossible for any wrestling fan over the age of 40 to forget the skills and theatrics of a four-foot, four-inch, 60-pound bundle of dynamite who went by the name Little Beaver. Resplendent in his Mohawk and full native dress, this Quebec-born-and-raised wrestler entertained fans for over four decades. During his peak years, his popularity rivalled that of any other big name in wrestling. In a sad note, in the biggest match of his career he was body-slammed by the 400-pound behemoth King Kong Bundy before 93,000 fans at Wrestlemania III. He suffered a serious back injury, and never appeared in the ring again. He died in 1995 at the age of 60.

14. Match these wrestling stars with the CFL teams they played for.

1) Tito Santana   a) Calgary Stampeders
2) Stu Hart   b) Montreal Alouettes
3) The Rock   c) Edmonton Eskimos
4) Lex Luger   d) British Columbia Lions

A. The answers are: 1 (d); 2 (c); 3 (a); 4 (b).

Santana, who was born Merced Solis, was a college gridiron standout at West Texas State. He played briefly for the Lions in the early '70s before committing himself to the ring wars, where he carved out a very respectable career for himself, winning the WWF's intercontinental belt. Hart was an offensive lineman for the Eskies back in the 1930s before hanging up his cleats in favour of wrestling. It turned out to be a wise decision, as Hart became one of the most influential people in the sport of wrestling. The Rock, aka Dwayne Johnson, played for the University of Miami before making a bid for the pro ranks. He only made it as far as the Stamps' practice squad before he switched to wrestling. He has not only become a superstar of WWE wrestling but is now also a much sought-after movie actor. Under his real name, Larry Pfohl, Luger was an offensive lineman for the Als between 1979 and 1981. He twice won the world championship in the WCW.

15. Which professional wrestling star has a hockey team named after him?

A. Bret "The Hitman" Hart can honestly say he has done it all in pro wrestling. This former champ in the WWF and WCW is the son of the legendary Stu Hart, and the most successful of the many Hart brothers who have donned wrestling tights over the years. In the late 1990s, he was part of the ownership group that brought major junior hockey to his hometown of Calgary, so it seemed natural that the team be called the Hitmen. Bret often wore a team sweater to public appearances, bringing the Hitmen a great deal of international exposure. Even though the franchise is now owned by the NHL's Calgary Flames, Brett still takes an active role in the club, attending many home games and boosting morale in the team's dressing room.

16. Which first family of Quebec wrestling has spawned four generations of successful grapplers?

A. With the possible exception of the Harts of Calgary, no family even comes close to matching the success and longevity of the Rougeaus, who have been great ambassadors for the sport of wrestling. Here are only a few highlights from amongst their many accomplishments.

Eddie Auger was a tough old-school wrestler who held regional titles for many years and later trained his two nephews, Johnny and Jacques Rougeau.

Johnny, who competed between 1952 and 1971, was one of the most popular wrestlers ever to don the tights in Quebec. He was also a famous restaurateur and club owner, as well as a very successful hockey executive. (He ran the Laval junior club that Mike Bossy played for, and since 1983 the Quebec Major Junior Hockey League has presented the John Rougeau Trophy to the team with the best regular-season record.)

Jacques Rougeau Sr. was a frequent tag-team partner of his big brother, but was also very popular in his own right. He last wrestled in the 1980s. His sons, Raymond and Jacques Jr., had great success as a tag team — as the Fabulous Rougeau Brothers, of course. They were local champs, but never held the WWF belt. Raymond is now the WWE's French-language commentator, while Jacques is still wrestling. He went on to become the WWF intercontinental champ, ran afoul of the RCMP when he adopted the character of "The Mountie," and finally won the tag-team title alongside Pierre-Carl Ouelette as "The Quebecers."

A third brother, Armand, showed great potential, but his career was cut short in the mid 1980s by a serious back injury.

Finally, there is J.J. Rougeau, now 15 years old, who is the son of Jacques Jr. and made his wrestling debut in 2001 in a family-run promotion.

17. What tie does NHL defenceman Denis Gauthier have with the world of professional wrestling?

A. If one look at his imposing frame (six feet two, 230 pounds) didn't tell you you'd have to be crazy to tangle with Gauthier, you'd be convinced of it after you learn that his uncles are Raymond, Jacques and Armand Rougeau. The Calgary Flames bruiser is the son of Joanne Rougeau, herself a very successful bodybuilder and wrestling executive. He was drafted in the first round (20th overall) by the Flames and has established himself as one of the most rugged checkers in the game.

18. Which family ran the sport of wrestling in Toronto for over 60 years?

A. As promoters, no one in Canada has wielded as much power as Toronto's own Frank, Jack and Eddie Tunney, who ruled the wrestling hotbed from the 1930s until the mid '90s. Family patriarch Frank got his start working for Jack Corcoran before taking over the promotional reins himself. He dealt with all the biggest names of the sport and made Toronto one of the greatest wrestling cities in the world. His advice and promotional skill helped make stars of such names as Whipper Watson, The Sheik and Lord Athol Layton. After his passing in 1983, the torch was picked up by his nephew Jack and son Eddie. Jack Tunney soon aligned himself with Vince McMahon Jr. and was a driving force behind the sport's transformation into a massive entertainment sensation in the late 1980s and early '90s. Jack Tunney held the title of president of the World Wrestling Federation for about a decade.

19. How many times has Canada hosted a Wrestlemania spectacular?

A. The brainchild of promoter extraordinaire Vince McMahon, Wrestlemania has, since its inception in 1985, become the largest annual extravaganza in the world of professional wrestling. On Sunday April 1, 1990, the Wrestlemania caravan rolled into Toronto and its state-of-the-art Skydome. A huge crowd of 67,678 packed its way into the venue to see the intercontinental champ, The Ultimate Warrior, pin the legendary Hulk Hogan to claim the world heavyweight belt. Skydome once again played host to the wrestling world on March 17, 2002, when an even bigger throng of 68,237 watched Triple H defeat Canada's Chris Jericho in the main event.

20. Which Canadian resident is known to all as "King Kong"?

A. Big Angelo Mosca came to Canada in the late 1950s. After a standout football career at Notre Dame, he caught on with the Hamilton Tiger-Cats, with whom he was part of four Grey Cup–winning teams. In the late '60s, Mosca began a second career as a professional wrestler, and the moniker of King Kong seemed natural for the six-foot, five-inch, 300-pound athlete. Extremely successful as a mat warrior, he also went on to add colour commentary, promoting and acting to his portfolio. Truly a gentle giant, Mosca is known to all as a generous man who has worked very hard on behalf of charities.

MISCELLANEOUS

1. Which Canadian soccer star was named North America's player of the year?

A. Born in Croatia and raised in Toronto, Branko Segota was one of the highest-scoring forwards in North American soccer history. This five-time all-star scored a total of 73 goals in 147 North American Soccer League games and added an amazing 12 goals in 13 playoff games. As a member of the Golden Bay Earthquakes, Segota was chosen as the NASL's player of the year in 1984. In 10 seasons of indoor soccer he potted an impressive 426 goals in 369 games. A member of the Canada's 1986 World Cup team, he was inducted into the Canadian Soccer Hall of Fame in 2002.

2. Which Canadian soccer star has twice been selected to the World All-Star team?

A. Ottawa's own Charmaine Hooper has, throughout the past decade, been one of the most dominant women soccer players in the world. A stalwart of the Canadian national team, Hooper has scored an impressive 62 goals in 115 games for Canada in international play. A graduate of North Carolina State, she was twice named to the All-America team by the National Soccer Coaches Association of America. In May 2004, she was named to the international all-star team that was chosen to play Germany, the defending World Cup women's champions, in an important friendly match that was part of FIFA's 100th anniversary celebrations.

3. Which Canadian player's rights did Everton of the English Premier League pay £4.5 million to obtain?

A. Born in Poland, raised in Canada, Tomasz Radzinski has become a star in England since 2001, when Everton opened the vault to acquire him from his old club, Anderlecht of Belgium. The transfer fee is reportedly the highest ever paid for a Canadian soccer player. Radzinski, started his pro career with St. Catharines Roma of the Canadian Professional Soccer League before moving to Belgium. He has scored more than 20 goals in his tenure with Everton, leading the side with 11 in 2002–03.

4. Which Calgary-born midfielder chose to play internationally for England instead of Canada?

A. As a star player for the Calgary Foothills club, Owen Hargreaves was discovered at the age of 15 by a German coach who recommended him to the powerful Bayern Munich organization. Since making the team in 1997, Hargreaves has made quite a name for himself. He also touched off a bit of controversy in 2001, when he elected to play for England's national team (he was eligible because his father was born in England) rather than his native Canada or Wales (his mother's homeland). At publication time he had played 19 games for England.

5. Which Canadian soccer goalie played in the English Premier League for Ipswich Town, Chelsea and West Ham?

A. It was Port Coquitlam, B.C.'s own Craig Forrest, who achieved the feat during his career play in England. One of the highlights of his 17-year career came in 1991–92, when his solid play helped Ipswich Town gain a promotion from the First Division to the Premiership. He played for Canada in two World Cup qualifying tournaments and was an important member of the team that won the CONCACAF Gold Cup in 2000. Forrest retired from soccer in 2002 and has done a fine job in his new career as a sportscaster in Canada. Showing great courage, he has also defeated testicular cancer.

6. Who was the last Canadian man to win the Boston Marathon?

A. It was Jerome Drayton, in 1977. Born in Germany, this proud Canadian citizen made a name for himself when he won the prestigious Fukuoka Marathon for the first time in 1969 (he would win it twice more). Besieged by injuries throughout his career, Drayton won a silver medal at the 1978 Commonwealth Games and placed sixth at the 1976 Olympics in Montreal. His time of 2 hours, 10 minutes and 8 seconds in the 1975 Canadian champions has yet to be bettered.

7. Which Canadian track and field star was successful stockbroker before becoming a world champion?

A. A great all-around athlete with a love for basketball, Donovan Bailey was making a great living as a stockbroker before he began training in earnest in 1994. He burst onto the scene in 1995, winning both the 100-metre and 4x100 relay at the world championships at Göteborg, Sweden. He repeated those wins at the 1996 Olympics in Atlanta, setting a world record of 9.84 seconds in the 100-metre race. The following year he won gold again at the worlds as part of the

4x100 relay team. Bothered by injuries, Donovan retired from running in 2001.

8. Which Canadian made a successful run across the country to raise money for cancer research?

A. On March 31, 1984, in St. John's, Newfoundland, Steve Fonyo began an epic 14-month, 8,000-kilometre journey across Canada. Born in Montreal, Steve lost part of his left leg to cancer at the age of 12. He decided to complete the run that Terry Fox had attempted, and had been forced to abandon at the halfway mark, four years earlier. By the time Steve's journey ended in Victoria, B.C., on May 29, 1985, Fonyo's run had raised $13 million for cancer research. In 1987, he was named to the Order of Canada. This true Canadian hero now makes his home in British Columbia.

9. Who was the first disabled athlete to be inducted into the Canadian Sports Hall of Fame?

A. Born in Saskatoon, Arnie Boldt lost his right leg at the age of three in a farm accident. This courageous athlete earned international attention in 1976 when, at the Toronto Paralympics, he not only won two gold medals but set world records by clearing 6 feet, 1¼ inches in the high jump and recording a 9-foot, 8½-inch long jump. Following those successes, he also won the same two events at the Canadian Games for the Physically Disabled and again in 1980 at the Paralympics in Arnhem in the Netherlands. On August 27, 1977, Arnie was inducted into the Canadian Sports Hall of Fame.

10. Who won the Canadian Press's female athlete of the year award in 2003?

A. At the 2003 World Track and Field Championships in Paris, Perdita Felicien set a new world record, blazing through the 100-metre hurdles in 12.53 seconds. Earlier that year, while running for the University of Illinois, the Pickering, Ontario, native won her second consecutive national collegiate title in the 100-metre hurdles, becoming the NCAA's female athlete of the year in track and field. And on January 5, 2004, it was announced that Felicien had been chosen for the CP honour. She was the first track athlete to win the prestigious award in 25 years.

11. Which Hollywood personality was discovered at a CFL game?

A. Wearing a Labatt's T-shirt as she sat in the stands at a 1989 game between the B.C. Lions and Toronto Argonauts, Pamela Anderson caught the attention of a cameraman, and her image was flashed on the B.C. Place scoreboard. The rest is history, of a sort, as she was launched on a career in modelling and commercials. The Vancouver-born Pam would then appear as a regular on *Home Improvement*, *Baywatch* and *VIP* and star in an infamous home video with ex-husband Tommy Lee. She has also appeared in *Playboy* magazine on numerous occasions and starred in the movie *Barb Wire*.

12. Which Canadian martial arts superstar is nicknamed "The Ronin"?

A. Newmarket, Ontario's Carlos Newton has, for the past several years, been one of the most successful and exciting fighters in the world of mixed martial arts. Few fans of the Ultimate Fighting Championships (UFC) could forget his submission chokehold win over long-time world champion Pat Miletich at UFC 31 to win the welterweight title. During his career, Newton has also defeated such notable martial artists as Pele, Renzo Gracie and Pete Spratt. Carlos is also the three-time Canadian jiujitsu champion, as well as Canada's national pankration champ.

13. Who is known as the North Bay Assassin?

Chantal Nadon

A. Pretty, petite Chantal Nadon looks like anything but the fierce competitor that she is in the world of martial arts. This fighting dynamo is the five-time world kickboxing champion. After winning the 1994 Ontario boxing championships, Chantal, who has a very extensive martial arts background, turned to the sport of professional kickboxing. In September of 1994 she made her pro debut, earning a draw with American veteran Sue Chase. Fighting all over the world, she won the first of her five world titles in September 1998. Trained by the famed Twin Dragons, Michael and Martin McNamara, Chantal — who is also married to Michael — is taking a sabbatical from the ring after giving birth to her daughter, Brigitte. Her professional record stands at 15 wins, 3 losses and 2 draws.

14. Who is known simply as "Sugarfoot"?

A. Edmonton native Pete Cunningham is known by that moniker because of his reputation as one of the greatest kickers ever in the sport of kickboxing. Cunningham went stateside early in his career to study under the tutelage of the legendary Benny "the Jet" Urquidez. This eight-time world champion has an incredible record of 50 wins, no losses and one draw, with 21 knockouts. On October 2, 1998, Sugarfoot was the very first person inducted into the ISKA Hall of Fame. The ISKA is the largest and most prestigious martial arts sanctioning body. Cunningham has also pursued a career as an actor and stuntman, appearing in such movies as *I Spy* and *Bloodfist 3* and TV shows like *Kung Fu* and *Walker, Texas Ranger*.

15. Has Canada ever won a world championship team karate event?

A. Actually, Canada's team boasts one of the finest records in the sport of karate. In 2002, at the World Kickboxing

Association's world championships in Marina di Massa, Italy, Canada won the overall team title when a delegation of 111 competitors won a total of 93 medals, 39 of them gold. This tournament is the largest of its kind, hosting 2,200 athletes from 37 countries. What makes this title even more impressive is that it marked the fifth time in a row that Canada had won this tournament.

16. What sport is Dominique Bosshart a champion in?

A. This Manitoba-raised woman is an absolute wrecking ball in the Olympic sport and martial art of tae kwon do. One of the world's premier practitioners, she has won 11 straight Canadian championships, beginning in 1993, when she was only 15 years old. She followed up a bronze medal win at the 1999 Pan American Games in Winnipeg by winning gold at the the 2000 Pan American Tae Kwon Do championships the next year. These successes led to her first Olympic appearance, at the Sydney Games, where she won bronze.

17. Has Canada ever had a world heavyweight champion in the sport of judo?

A. Yes, indeed. In October 2001, Montreal's Nicolas Gill defeated the defending Olympic gold medallist, Antal Kovacs of Hungary, to win the first-ever Professional Grand Prix Judo Championships. Gill has won close to a dozen Canadian championships throughout his career and was the silver medal winner at the 2000 Olympic Games in Sydney. The six-foot, one-inch, 225-pound martial artist has also won gold at the 2002 Commonwealth Games and the 2001 Francophone Games.

18. Has a Canadian man ever won a major international tennis tournament?

A. Yes, but it was quite some time ago. Even though Canada has developed a number of strong tennis players in the past, the nation has never been considered a world powerhouse in the sport. In 1935, Bob Murray of Montreal won the Scottish Open to become the first Canadian ever to win a major tennis tournament. A graduate of McGill University and an intercollegiate champion, Murray played at Wimbledon in 1935 and '36 and captained Canada's Davis Cup squad.

19. Can you name the Academy Award–nominated actor who once played football for the Toronto Argonauts?

A. Nominated for his work in the 1938 movie *Algiers*, Gene Lockhart was one of the finest dramatic actors of his time. The native of London, Ontario was also applauded for his stage work, particularly his portrayal of Willie Loman in Arthur Miller's classic play, *Death of a Salesman*. A fine athlete in his youth, he won a national one-mile swim meet in 1909 and played football for the Argos from 1910 to 1912. He was also the father of actress June Lockhart, of *Lassie* and *Lost in Space* fame.

20. What other sport did Canadian skating queen Barbara Ann Scott have great success in?

A. After winning at the world championships in 1947 and both the worlds and the Winter Olympics in '48, Scott turned pro, performing in ice shows, but the nomadic lifestyle didn't agree with her. Marrying the publicity agent for the Hollywood Ice Revue, she retired from skating and took up training show horses, becoming one of the finest equestrians in North America. Also, in the past number of years she has returned to figure skating as a judge at international tournaments.

21. Who was the first Canadian to successfully go over Niagara Falls?

A. There seems to be some debate over this question. Many seem to believe that it was "Smiling" Jean Lussier who first accomplished the feat, on July 4, 1928. It is said that Lussier was born and raised in the province of Quebec, but there are detractors who believe that Lussier was actually from Springfield, Massachusetts, and was the grandson of Quebecers.

Some believe that it was actually Karel Soucek of Hamilton, Ontario, who was the first Canuck to conquer the Falls, on July 3, 1985. Soucek was killed a year later, trying to re-create the feat at the Houston Astrodome. The idea was that his barrel would be dropped from the top of the dome, 180 feet above the stadium floor, and land in the middle of a huge tank of water. Instead, it hit the rim of the tank and he sustained mortal injuries.

22. Was the first televised hockey game in Canada in English or French?

A. On October 11, 1952, television station CBFT transmitted the very first game, between the Montreal Canadiens and Detroit Red Wings, with commentary *en français*. The first English-language telecast was beamed over Toronto station CBLT 19 days later. That game featured the hometown Toronto Maple Leafs and the Boston Bruins. But both of these Canadian telecasts came 12 years after station W2XBS, a New York experimental station owned by NBC, carried a game between the Rangers and Canadiens on February 25, 1940.

23. Has Canada ever won a world title in the sport of badminton?

A. Dorothy Walton, the pride of Swift Current, Saskatchewan, was a tremendous athlete who, as a student at the University of Saskatchewan, was a member of 14 different sports clubs. She was the first woman at the university to be honoured as its outstanding athlete. Moving to Toronto, she won her first provincial badminton title in 1935, then was victorious in both the Canadian and North American championships. In 1939, she won the All-England badminton championship, which was recognized as the world title. The tournament was suspended during the war years, so Dorothy's reign was extended until competition resumed in 1947.

24. What sport has Roland Green become a world champion in?

A. Roland Green of Victoria, B.C., has become one of the great stars in the growing sport of mountain biking. After his breakthrough season in 2000, when he placed second at the world championships, Roland has become the man to beat in the sport. The winner of back-to-back world titles in 2001 and 2002 was also named Male MTB (mountain bike) Racer of the Year in 2002 by the *Cycling News*.

25. Which nation won the inaugural World Indoor Lacrosse Championship?

A. If it had been any country other than Canada, would there have been a place for the question in this book? The first worlds of indoor lacrosse were played in southern Ontario in May 2003 and were attended by teams from Australia, the Czech Republic, Scotland, the United States and the Iroquois Nationals (made up of indigenous players from the Six Nations–Iroquois Confederacy). Games were played in Oshawa, Mississauga, Kitchener and Hamilton. Canada defeated the Iroquois Nationals 21–4 in the final game, played at Hamilton's Copps Coliseum.

26. What did professional wrestler Jacques Rougeau and the Vancouver Grizzlies of the NBA have in common?

A. Rougeau had wrestled in the World Wrestling Federation (now the WWE) as a character called "The Mountie," dressed in a scarlet tunic. The Royal Canadian Mounted Police took offence and made the grappler stop. When the Grizzlies were applying for their NBA franchise, management considered calling the team the Vancouver Mounties. In negotiations with the RCMP, the real-life Mounties let it be known they were opposed, and the team became the Grizzlies.

27. What sport did Merv Deckert become a world champion in?

A. Winnipeg native Merv Deckert has often been called the Wayne Gretzky or Tiger Woods of the sport of handball. Now in his mid 50s and still dominating the seniors' circuit, he has held several key positions with handball associations and is very involved in promoting the sport. Athletics also run in the Deckert family; Merv's son Jesse is a very highly touted goalie in the Western Hockey League.

28. Which Canadian sport's champions are presented with the Mann Cup?

A. Donated to Canada's national sport of lacrosse by Sir Donald Mann in 1910, the Mann Cup is reportedly made of solid gold. Mann, one of the most influential men in Canada, was the builder of the Canadian Northern Railway. The trophy is presented to the nation's senior amateur champions, and the

New Westminster Salmonbellies have been the most frequent winners — their 24 titles are more than triple the number won by the next most successful team. The Cup made headlines in 1989, when it was stolen from its showcase at the Canadian Lacrosse Hall of Fame in New Westminster. Since its return, special security measures have been taken to protect it.

29. One of the most popular movies of 2003 was *Seabiscuit*, based on the story of the legendary racehorse. What was the Canadian connection to this story?

A. Seabiscuit's primary jockey was Edmonton-born Johnny "Red" Pollard. Pretty much a journeyman, he connected with Seabiscuit's trainer, Tom Smith, and history was made. Tall for a jockey at five feet, seven inches, Red was also passionate about the sport of boxing and had numerous battles in the squared circle. Unfortunately, he was also injury-plagued throughout his career; in particular, a serious leg injury prevented him from riding the Biscuit in the famous 1938 match race against the great War Admiral. Pollard returned to ride Seabiscuit to victory in the lucrative Santa Anita Handicap in 1940, after which the horse was retired. Pollard retired in 1955.

30. Sir Barton, the first horse ever to win the Triple Crown, also had a strong Canadian connection. What was it?

A. This great horse, which won the Kentucky Derby, Preakness, and Belmont Stakes in 1919, was owned by Commander J.K.L. Ross of Montreal, a well-known coal-mining tycoon. Sir Barton's Triple Crown is all the more impressive when you realize that, in 1919, the Derby and the Preakness were held only four days apart. Commander Ross was a fine all-around athlete in his own right, playing competitive hockey and collegiate football. He also commanded a ship in World War I, and donated a handful of large yachts to the Royal Canadian Navy. For his distinguished naval service, he was named to the Order of British Empire.

31. The Canadian Press didn't name a male or female athlete of the year for 1999? How come?

A. In this, the final year of the 20th century, CP's judges were busy choosing Canada's male and female athletes of the *century*. Their choices: the Great One himself, Wayne Gretzky, and Nancy Greene of British Columbia, who won many national and international titles, including a gold and a silver medal at the 1968 Winter Games in Grenoble, France.

32. The CP's male and female athlete-of-the-year awards are named for a pair of famous Canadians. Can you name them?

A. The men's trophy is named after the great Lionel Conacher, who was not only a successful athlete in more than half a dozen professional and amateur sports but was also an admired and respected provincial and federal politician. The women's prize is named after the great Fanny "Bobbie" Rosenfeld, who also excelled at every sport she tried. She enjoyed her greatest success in track and field, winning a gold medal in the 4x100 relay and a silver in the 100-metre sprint at the 1928 Olympics in Amsterdam. She also went on to become a very successful journalist.

33. Which Canadian tennis great won the CP's female athlete of the year award more often: Carling Bassett or Helen Kelesi?

A. This is a trick question. "Darling Carling" and "Hurricane Helen" were two of the greatest tennis players Canada ever produced, and both won the coveted Fanny Rosenfeld Award twice in their illustrious careers. Bassett won the award in 1983 and '85, while Kelesi claimed back-to-back honours in 1989 and 1990. Both are well behind the pace set by golfer Marlene Stewart Streit, who won a total of five times.

34. Which Canadian auto racer won the 2003 Fran-Am North American championship?

A. That would be the 17-year-old sensation, Andrew Ranger of Roxton Pond, Quebec. What made the achievement even more incredible was that 2003 was Ranger's first season driving race cars. The rookie won five times and was on the podium in nine of the 13 races in the Fran-Am series. A two-time Canadian karting champion, this young athlete seems to have a brilliant future ahead of him in the sport of auto racing.

35. Which Hall of Fame lacrosse player was also an NHL star and a politician?

A. Wilfred "Bucko" McDonald was one of those natural athletes who excelled in just about every sport he played. This native of Fergus, Ontario, played lacrosse for the Mann Cup champion Brampton Excelsiors and was well known as a referee and executive. He was inducted into the Canadian Lacrosse Hall of Fame in 1971. He was also one of the greatest defensive blueliners in hockey during his career with the New York Rangers and Toronto Maple Leafs. After retiring from athletics, he sought and won public office as a provincial and federal member of Parliament. Bucko also holds a special place in history as the coach who converted a very young Bobby Orr into a defenceman.

36. In what sport is Alison Sydor a three-time world champion?

A. Born in Edmonton, Alison has, over the past decade or so, become the top mountain biker in the world. Along with the silver medal she won at the 1996 Olympics in Atlanta, she won three consecutive World Mountain Bike Championships in 1994, '95 and '96. An accomplished multi-sport athlete, she is a race-winning triathlete and a competitive hockey player. She also sports a degree in biochemistry from the University of Victoria. Now a resident of North Vancouver, B.C., Sydor was chosen as the CP's Canadian female athlete of the year in 1996.

37. What sport did Sarah Thompson set a world record in?

A. Without a doubt, Sarah is one of the most dedicated and inspirational athletes in the world. Born in Picton, Ontario, this always-athletic woman lost her sight after the birth of her second child. Then, in 1974, she suffered a stroke that weakened her right side. Working hard in rehab, she discovered sports for the blind, and soon thereafter became an elite blind athlete. At the Canadian championships in 1982, she set national records in the 100-metre dash, long jump, discus, javelin and shotput. In 1987, she was named Ontario's Blind Athlete of the Year, and in 1990, competing in the masters division, she set world records in the squat, bench press and dead lift.

38. Can you name the five-time Canadian female arm-wrestling champion?

A. Born and raised on a dairy farm in Kingsbury, Quebec, Josée Marie Morneau was a natural athlete who excelled in track and field in high school. Always a powerful girl, this five-foot-seven, 175-pound powerhouse has long been attracted to strength sports. She has competed in many different arm-wrestling, strong-woman and Highland Games events, and won her division at the 2001 Canadian Highland Games. Josée has been a finalist in the World's Strongest Woman events in 2001, 2002 and 2003.

39. Can you match these nicknames to the Canadian athlete?

1) The Rifle	**a) Angelo Mosca**
2) The Entertainer	**b) Fanny Rosenfeld**
3) King Kong	**c) Arturo Gatti**
4) Bobbie	**d) Sam Etcheverry**
5) Thunder	**e) Eddie Shack**

A. The answers are: 1 (d); 2 (e); 3 (a); 4 (b); 5 (c).

Sam Etcheverry was one of the top quarterbacks in CFL history, hence the nickname "the Rifle." Eddie Shack was one of the most colourful players to ever play hockey. His on-ice antics made him a worthy recipient of the moniker "the Entertainer." Mosca was one of the most intimidating men ever to play pro football or enter the wrestling ring. Fanny Rosenfeld was one of the greatest athletes ever to represent Canada, as well as a great journalist and a pioneer in gay rights. Gatti, one of the finest Canadian boxers ever, is also known as the "Human Highlight Reel."

40. What sport has young Jennifer Spalding become a champion in?

A. A Vancouver native, Jennifer is one of the finest competitors in the sport of sailing. Winning many youth championships across Canada, as well as the gold medal at the 2001 Canada Summer Games, has put this athlete at the forefront of her sport. In recognition of all her successes in 2002, she was chosen as Canada's junior female athlete of the year.

41. Did a Canadian athlete ever lose a championship for "mooning"?

A. It happened at the 2001 Canada Summer Games, when Daniel Blouin of Quebec won a bronze medal in the 3,000-metre steeplechase. Caught up in the excitement of his high placing, he briefly mooned a group of his Quebec teammates. The Canada Games officials were not amused, and they stripped Blouin of his medal. Quebec team officials sent Blouin home to prevent the incident from being a distraction to the other athletes.

42. How many Canadians have been inducted into the World Golf Hall of Fame in St. Augustine, Florida?

A. Only one. In April 2004, the pride of Cereal, Alberta, Marlene Stewart Streit, became the first Canadian ever inducted into this most prestigious club. Playing exclusively as an amateur, she won the 1956 U.S. women's amateur championship and many other international and Canadian titles. An amazing highlight of her illustrious career took place in 2003, when, at the age of 69, she won her third USGA senior women's amateur title, 47 years after winning the U.S. women's amateur championship.

43. How many times has Karen Magnussen been the Canadian Press's choice as female athlete of the year?

A. Once. Throughout its sporting history, Canada has, not surprisingly, been one of the world's top nations in the sport of figure skating. One of the most popular Canadian skaters was a pretty young lady from Vancouver who had been performing for audiences since the age of six. In 1973, she won the world championships in Czechoslovakia, an achievement that warranted her selection as Canada's female athlete of the year.

Karen Magnussen

44. What sport is Canadian Jasey-Jay Anderson a world champion in?

A. A native of Mont-Tremblant, Quebec, Anderson is considered by most to be the top male snowboarder in the world today. Known for his intensity and fearless style on the hills, Anderson is the five-time FIS (International Ski Federation) Crystal Globes world champion. He has also won numerous national championships and the 2001 world alpine title. One of his most disappointing moments occurred at the 1998 Winter Olympics in Nagano, when the heavily favoured Anderson fell during the giant slalom event and finished 16th.

45. What sport was Mary "Bonnie" Baker a star in?

A. A native of Regina, Saskatchewan, Mary Baker was an all-star catcher in the All-American Girls' Professional Baseball League. Playing seven seasons with the South Bend Blue Sox, Mary became not only one of the finest players in the league but one of its biggest gate attractions. Her sister, Gene McFaul, was also a player in the league and was a teammate of Mary's in 1947. The movie *A League of Their Own* was a largely fictionalized account of the league, but it is reported that one of the film's leading characters — Dottie Hinson, played by Geena Davis — was based on Mary Baker.

46. Which Canadian rodeo star passed away while competing in 2002?

A. Kenny McLean was truly one of the greats in the world of saddle broncing. Born in Penticton, British Columbia, he got his start in rodeo by breaking colts for his father, and he officially launched his rodeo career at 17. Quickly becoming a force on the circuit, Kenny was named the world's rookie of the year in 1961. He followed that up in 1962 by winning the world saddle broncing championship. Five times a Canadian saddle bronc champ, he also became a top executive with the Professional Rodeo Cowboys Association. Tragically, the always-competitive McLean, a member of the B.C. Sports Hall of Fame and the Order of Canada, suffered a fatal heart attack at a seniors' event in Taber, Alberta, on July 13, 2002.

47. Which Canadian woman is a two-time world champion triathlete?

A. Lori Bowden of Victoria, B.C., won the Ironman World Championships in 1999 and 2003. Although she'd long been involved in the sport, it wasn't until the mid 1990s that Lori began to take these gruelling competitions seriously. Once she did, she quickly made a name for herself; within a couple of years she had won the Canadian championship. She is married to fellow Ironman champion — and Canadian — Peter Reid, in a union that some in the press corps have dubbed the "World's Fittest Couple."

48. What sport are the Turcotte sisters champions of?

A. Maryse and Karine Turcotte are a force in the sport of weightlifting. Older sister Maryse has been a trailblazer in the sport, breaking more than 50 provincial and national records so far in her career. This elite athlete, who competes in the 58-kilo category, is also the very first woman in North America ever to lift twice her body weight. Younger sister Karine started at the sport at the age of 16, when her sister's club desperately needed an extra member for a competition. Competing in the 48-kilo category, Karine made her major international breakthrough at the 2002 Commonwealth Games, when she came home with three silver medals.

49. Who is the highest-paid sports announcer in Canada?

A. That honour would appear to belong to none other than Don "Grapes" Cherry. Estimates vary, but the former coach of the Boston Bruins and Colorado Rockies, a veteran of a lone NHL game and more than 1,000 in the minor-leagues, pulls down anywhere from $500,000 to $700,000 a year for his work on "Coach's Corner." Next on the list would be Ron MacLean, the host of *Hockey Night in Canada* and Cherry's foil on "Coach's Corner," at about $450,000. A 2002 article in the *Globe and Mail* reported that Brian Williams, also of the CBC, brings home roughly $350,000 a year, an amount that increases during Olympic years, when Williams anchors the network's coverage of the Summer and Winter Games.

50. Which sports was Velma Springstead of Hamilton, Ontario, associated with?

A. In the 1920s, when organized women's sports were in their infancy, Velma was a high jumper and hurdler. In the summer of 1925 she qualified for the first Canadian women's team to take part in international competition. At a meet in England, Springstead was third in the high jump and fourth in the hurdles, but her infectious joy and team spirit made an indelible impression on many of those present, inspiring Lord Decies to present her with a special trophy. Sadly, she didn't live to fulfill her athletic potential, as she died of pneumonia in March 1926, at the age of only 19. But her memory lives on, as the female athlete of the year award commissioned in 1932 and currently presented by the Spirit of Sport Foundation bears her name.

51. Which Canadian hero wheeled himself around the world to raise awareness of disabilities?

A. In 1973, Rick Hansen was an active, athletic 15-year-old when his whole world changed after a car crash left him a paraplegic. Always a determined fighter, Rick bounced back and began an extremely successful sporting career that saw him win 19 wheelchair marathons, including three world championships. He also competed at the 1984 Paralympic Games in Los Angeles. In the spring of 1985, Rick began his Man in Motion world tour, which saw him travel more than 40,000 kilometres in his wheelchair over the next two years. Along the way, he met with world leaders, celebrities and the Pope to bring attention to all that can be accomplished by the disabled. Today he is president and CEO of the Rick Hansen Man in Motion Foundation, which strives to improve the lives of people with spinal-cord injuries.

52. What sport is Christine Nordhagen a world champion in?

A. Few Canadian athletes have dominated their sport as amateur wrestler Christine Nordhagen of Calgary has. Born on a large farm in Valhalla, Alberta, Christine discovered the sport while a phys. ed. major at the University of Calgary. This 10-time Canadian champion in the 72-kilo weight class is the most highly decorated female wrestler in the world today. Winning a total of six gold medals at the world championships, Nordhagen has also won two golds at the Pan American Games. She is a solid favourite to win gold at the 2004 Olympics in Athens, where women's wrestling is making its debut.

53. Which thoroughbred jockey was twice chosen as Canada's top athlete?

A. Oshawa, Ontario's Sandy Hawley received the Lou Marsh Trophy in 1973 and again in 1976. Starting his career in

Sandy Hawley

1968, he was chosen as North America's top apprentice a year later. In '73, Hawley became the first North American rider to break the 500-win barrier, ending up with 515 victories, shattering the 20-year-old record of 485 set by racing legend Bill Shoemaker. He led North American jockeys in wins in 1970, '72, '73 and '76. He won the Queen's Plate race four times and remained one of the sport's top jockeys until his retirement in 1998. Hawley was awarded the Order of Canada and is a member of the Canadian Sports Hall of Fame.

54. Which legendary Canadian swimmer was elected to the Ontario provincial parliament?

Cindy Nicholas

A. It was Toronto's own "Queen of the Channel," Cindy Nicholas, who represented the riding of Scarborough Centre in the legislature from 1987 until 1990. She served on several committees and chaired the Standing Committee on the Ombudsman. She now has a thriving law practice in Toronto and is often asked to lend her experience and advice to young swimmers. In 1974, at the age of 16, Cindy became the fastest swimmer ever to cross Lake Ontario, and 30 years later she still holds the women's record. A year later, she crossed the English Channel for the first time, and became the first woman to make a round trip. When she retired, she had crossed the Channel 19 times — which was then a world record. Since then, Alison Streeter of England has more than doubled her total.

Edward Zawadzki's

sporting endeavours have seen him in many roles, from university football player to columnist to boxing promoter and kickboxing commentator. He currently lives in Toronto. *The Ultimate Canadian Sports Trivia Book Volume II,* is Zawadzki's second book.